Anonymous

The first Indian member of the Imperial Parliament

Anonymous

The first Indian member of the Imperial Parliament

ISBN/EAN: 9783337153199

Printed in Europe, USA, Canada, Australia, Japan

Cover: Foto ©Suzi / pixelio.de

More available books at **www.hansebooks.com**

THE FIRST INDIAN MEMBER

OF THE

IMPERIAL PARLIAMENT,

BEING

A COLLECTION OF THE MAIN INCIDENTS

RELATING TO THE ELECTION OF

MR. DADABHAI NAOROJI to Parliament.

Price : Re. 1, Postage 1 anna extra.

Madras:

PRINTED BY ADDISON AND CO. MOUNT ROAD.

1892.

PREFACE.

It is superfluous to say anything by way of apology or justification for the publication of this little book. In the ever-memorable connection of India with England, there is perhaps no event which attests more strongly or more remarkably to the evergrowing cosmopolitanism of English life and the philanthropy of English character than the election by the electors of Cental Finsbury of an Indian gentleman to represent their interests in the greatest national assembly of the world. The suffrages of the Finsbury electors exercised in the spirit of broad, supra-insular sympathy have not only secured to themselves a faithful and conscientious arbiter of their interests, but have also been the means of indirectly transmitting both to the 'sputtering' and voiceless millions of India a friendly message, that for once in the annals of English political life will be added to the few ardent and disinterested advocates of Indian reform in the House the characteristically native ring of the voice of the patriot. The spontaneous rejoicings in all parts of India that immediately followed this memorable event have a three-fold significance, *first*, that one of India's sons has been found to be possessed of the culture and general qualifications as to be acceptable to a section of the English people, who, with their traditional cautious instincts, and but for the severe test to which they have put him during a long and trying period, would have been slow to recognize any assimilation of alien with local interests; *secondly*, that the revered and historic sanctotum, not only of English but of universal liberty, the asylum of the oppressed and forlorn in all quarters of the globe should entertain within its walls one who, notwithstanding ethnic differences of opinion, is one of our own, and who has so far, by dint of indomitable perseverance, assailed the medley of sneers, indignation, infuriated disappoint. ment, and unsavoury sarcasm of 'The English Parliament and the Black Man' by the thorough falsifier of concrete result achieved; and *thirdly*, that Indian wants and Indian aspirations will find a safe and certain medium of communication with the British public, unclouded by misrepresentations and deriving new force from the credibility and infallibility which attach to one who speaks with the confidence of a long and perfect acquaintanceship. If Anglo-Indian administration in India has hitherto afforded ample proofs of its spirit of benevolence in a wide and extensive distribution of patronage to indigenous culture and in the free scope given to native public opinion to exert its influence in its councils of deliberation and in kindred acts of generous statesmanship, its mainspring in England has carried this spirit to its picturesque perfection by recognizing Indian claims to higher and more exalted spheres of work, to guide the destinies of the Empire on which it has been truly said 'the sun never set.' broad based on the expanded brotherhood of a common humanity.

As to the gentleman himself who forms the hero of this little book, it is needless to expatiate at any length. The highest praise that can be accorded to him has but too clearly proved its deservedness in the memorable incident with which his name will inseparably be associated ; the results of high culture, long services of usefulness to his country, and a uniform disposition of sympathy have attained their fruition in an elevation which, apart from its merits of distinction, gives to one who is so inclined the means of doing good to half the world.

This little book is, in its own humble way, intended to perpetuate the memory of this important incident. It does not pretend to be exhaustive of *all* the circumstances connected with Mr. Dadabhai Naoroji's election to Parliament. Having regard to the impatience generally exhibited by readers to go through dry and uninteresting details, added to the difficulty of procuring all the requisite materials that may perhaps give a cheery and attractive shape to the work, the compilers had necessarily to restrict it to the compass of a small book detailing only the main incidents that may prove to be of interest and be consistent with light and leisurely reading. For any shortcomings in the execution of our plans, we crave indulgent treatment by our readers.

THE COMPILERS.

MADRAS, }
23rd December 1892. }

CONTENTS.

A Sketch of Mr. Dadabhai Naoroji's Past Career.

(EXTRACTED FROM THE *Bombay Gazette*.)

" FROM his early years Mr. Dadabhai showed himself to be a bright boy. He was generally the Exhibition boy, both in vernacular and the English schools. On one occasion, in the Government English school, another boy of his class carried off the prize in mental arithmetic by preparing most of the ready-reckoner by heart; but at the public exhibition for the distribution of prizes, the prize-boy broke down, when the little ' Dady ' stepped to the front, regained his first place, and there and then won his prize from one of the spectators. It is of this incident, we believe, that Mrs. Poston, in her ' Western India,' speaks regarding the little Parsee lad ' with an over-hanging forehead, and small sparkling eyes, peculiarly attracting our attention. The moment a question was proposed to the class, he quickly took a step before the rest, contracted his brows in deep and anxious thought, and with parted lips and finger eagerly uplifted towards the master, silently but rapidly worked his problem in a manner peculiar to himself, and blurted out the solution with a startling haste, half painful, half ludicrous. The little fellow seemed wholly animated with the desire of excelling, and his mental capabilities promised him a rich reward.' In 1845 Sir Erskine Perry, Chief Justice of Bombay, and President of the Board of Education, with his general desire to promote education among the natives, proposed to send Mr. Dadabhai to England to study for the Bar, offering to contribute half the expenses himself, and asking Sir Jamsetjee Jeejeebhoy, the first Baronet, and other *shetts*, to give the other half. The proposal was at first accepted, but was subsequently declined; and the general report of the reason was that somebody had frightened Sir Jamsetjee that young Dadabhai might be tempted to become a Christian in England, as a few years previously there had been much excitement among the Parsees on account of some conversions to Christianity. Soon afterwards Mr.

Dadabhai was appointed head native assistant master, and, on the occasion of the annual exhibition for the distribution of prizes, was declared by Principal Harkness to be entitled to the gold medal of the year. His subsequent career as Assistant Professor and Professor of Mathematics and Natural Philosophy in the Elphinstone College, in succession to Professor Patton, was successful and satisfactory. The distinction of Assistant Professor was conferred upon him in consideration of his great usefulness as well as of his very high character. Every successive Professor had borne testimony to the extent of his acquirements, as well as to his zeal and energy; and the Board of Education testified to the repeated opportunities of observing his 'devotion to the cause of native education.' Mr. Dadabhai was the first Native Professor, not only in Bombay, but in all India; and the Board of Education, in their report for 1854-55, referred to his appointment in these terms—' To complete the arrangements, we gladly availed ourselves of the opportunity of confirming Mr. Dadabhai Naoroji as Professor of Mathematics and Natural Philosophy, the duties of which he had been performing to our entire satisfaction for nearly two years. We feel sure that the distinction he has thus won by a long and laborious devotion to Mathematical studies, and by an able discharge of his duties in the instruction, will stimulate him to still greater exertion. It is now twenty-eight years since the subject of the Elphinstone Professorships first came under consideration, with the view of commemorating the high sense entertained by the natives of Western India of the public and private character of the Hon. Mountstuart Elphinstone on his retirement from the government of this Presidency. At a public meeting held in the Library of the Native Education Society in August 1827, a resolution was unanimously passed that the most appropriate and durable plan for accomplishing this object would be to found Professorships for teaching the English language, and the arts, the sciences, and the literature of Europe. In the resolution which was thus adopted, a hope was expressed that the happy period would arrive when natives of this country would be found qualified for holding those Professorships. It was, therefore, with no ordinary feeling of satisfaction that we felt ourselves justified in nominating Mr. Dadabhai Naoroji to the chair of Mathematics and Natural Philosophy—a measure so entirely in accordance with both the letter and spirit of the resolution. On another occasion, Dr. M. Stovell, Secretary of the Board of Education, wrote to Mr. Dadabhai a letter of congratulation and advice, telling him to ' go on in the same steady, straightforward course, and with the same single-minded views, and you may prove in time a great blessing to your countrymen.'

" During his educational career, and before his visits to England, Mr. Dadabhai did not confine his energies to his own regular work, but was either one of the originators of, or an active labourer in, most of the public movements of the time. The Students' Literary and Scientific Society, the Dnyan Prasarak Society, the Bombay Association, the Rahnoomœ Mazdiasna Society (for religious reforms among the Parsees), the Framjee Cowasjee Institute, the lrance Fund, the Parsee Gymnasium, the Widow Remarriage Movement among the Hindoos, the Victoria and Albert Museum, and the first girls' school of the Students' Literary and Scientific Society were indebted to him as an originator or active labourer for their success and advancement. In the cause of female education he threw his whole heart and soul; and he was spoken of by those who had watched and known his anxious work as 'the father of the girls' schools.' In the infancy of the movement a few volunteer teachers from the members of the Students' Society had at first opened the schools at their own houses, and were teaching during their leisure hours in the morning. In all his work Mr. Dadabhai esteemed and respected his fellow-workers, and they in turn worked under his lead with pleasure and unanimity. Much of the success of the Parsee Law Association in England in persuading the Law Commissioners and the Secretary of State for India to grant the special legislation asked for was due to the joint exertions of Mr. Dadabhai and Mr. Nowrozjee Furdoonjee. Mr. Dadabhai was the president of the ' Native Literary Society' which was incorporated with the Students' Literary and Scientific Society in the year 1848. He was vice-president and treasurer of the latter Society, and one of the volunteer teachers and superintendents of the Society's female schools. He was president of the Guzeratee Dnyan Prasarak Society for four or five years; secretary of the Rahnoomœ Mazdiasna Society for two or three years; one of the promoters and a member of the committee of the

Bombay Association; and one of the promoters and on the committee of the Framjee Cowasjee Institute. He took an active part in the success of the Iranee Fund, raised for ameliorating the condition of the Zoroastrians resident in Persia; and in the settlement of the trust of the Fort Charitable Dispensary. He took an active interest in the success of the Parsee Gymnasium, and drafted a set of rules for its management, which were adopted. He projected the Canning Fellowship, which, unfortunately, owing to the commercial crisis, was allowed to fall through. Mr. Dadabhai was among the first of those to propose a statue to Sir Jamsetjee Jeejeebhoy, the first Baronet, and was largely instrumental in carrying through the proposal for a statue of the Hon. Jugannath Sunkersett. Mr. Dadabhai's connection with journalism dates as far back as 1851, when he contributed to the *Samachar Durpan*, a daily Gujeratee newspaper, a series of articles with the title ' Dialogue between Socrates and Diogenes.' In order to hold the various public movements in which he took a share, and to introduce a higher style and tone of journalism among the Parsees, Mr. Dadabhai in the year 1851 started the *Rast Goftar* newspaper, which he edited for two years without any remuneration, and paid others for editing it when he could not write for want of time. The amount of literary work he went through was highly creditable to his industry. He contributed to the Dnyan Prasrak Magazine some eighteen lectures on National Philosophy and Astronomy, which had been delivered at meetings of the Society of that name, as well as papers on different social subjects. Before the Students' Literary and Scientific Society he read several papers and delivered lectures. In the Sir Jamsetjee Jeejeebhoy Philosophic Institute he delivered a lecture on Astronomy. As secretary of the Rahnoomae Society, he worked with the president, Mr. Nowrozjee Furdoonjee, in editing its periodical publications, and wrote one or two papers himself. While a discussion was going on on the subject of introducing native ladies at dinners and social gatherings, Mr. Dadabhai wrote an account of the condition of women in different countries in past times, which was subsequently published in a local newspaper. With these and other burdens upon him, he could yet find time to learn several languages; for he has a knowledge, besides English, of French, Persian, Hindustani, Gujeratee, and Marathi.

" When the project of starting the first native mercantile firm in England was taken up by the Camas, Mr. Dadabhai was offered a share in the firm, though he never had the least experience as a merchant. He accepted the offer solely because he was desirous to promote a more intimate and personal connection between England and India, and more especially to make a home for young natives to go to England for education and competition for the Indian Civil and Medical Services, which were then recently thrown open. ' India for the Indians ' was then, as now, his aim. But for this he would not have exchanged mathematics for merchandise. He first went to England in 1885, and has spent well-nigh twenty years there, returning to Bombay from time to time as the exigencies of his own and public business required. While in England he imposed upon himself the anxious and arduous task of making Englishmen take an active interest in Indian questions, and to read papers on Indian subjects. It was this silent work to which he had for a time to devote much perseverance, energy, tact, and some money. He persuaded many friends in Bombay and elsewhere to send their sons to England, and took upon himself their guardianship. He has now the satisfaction of seeing numbers of natives visiting England for education, business, profession, or travelling. Many a native who has visited England will remember his ever-ready help, advice, and kindness. As a merchant, Mr. Dadabhai has always been respected for his straightforwardness and honesty in all his dealings and business relations ; and so far was he then respected and esteemed that when in trying to extricate a mercantile friend from his embarrassments, he lost three lakhs of rupees, and owing to large failures in Bombay, his own firm failed, his creditors deeply sympathised with him, and not only released him within a few weeks, but helped him by engaging his services in the liquidation ; while some friends at once gave him new loans to set him up in business again. Much public sympathy was expressed for him at the time. Mr. Sorabjee Shapurjee Bengalee, c.i.e., refers, in his lately published book, to an incident illustrative of the high commercial character Messrs. Dadabhai Naoroji and Co. enjoyed in England. One or two Indian banks having attempted to hold back documents, the drafts of which Messrs. Dadabhai Naoroji and Co. were ready to pay, Mr. Dadabhai at once stoutly resisted the attempt by raising a controversy in the *Times;* and the Governor of the Bank of England saw Mr. Dadabhai at his office and complimented him on his spirited resistance and the justness of his contest. While in England Mr. Dadabhai was connected with several public bodies, and was a member of the Liverpool Literary and Philosophic Society, of the Philomathic Society, and of the Council of the Liverpool Athenæum; a member of the Cotton Supply Association of Manchester, of the Royal Institution of London, of the Royal Asiatic Society of Great Britain and Ireland, of the Ethnological and Anthropological Societies of the Society of Arts, and the National Indian Association. He was also president of the London Indian Society and honorary secretary of the East India Association. He was appointed Professor of Gujaratee in the London University College and a member of its Senate; and was director of the Queen Insurance Company, and a guarantor of the Exhibition of 1862. He was highly respected as a Mason as he was as a man and a merchant. He was secretary and one of the founders of the Lodge named 'Marquis of Dalhousie,' and is one of its past masters. He made a speech at the Mansion House on the occasion of a subscription fund raised for India. In 1859 he corresponded with Lord Stanley, then Secretary of State for India, on the subject of the Civil Service rules, which ended in an assurance given to Mr. Dadabhai that no further changes in the regulations would at any time be made without early publicity being given to them. In 1860 he spoke at a public meeting at Manchester on the cotton supply, and his address was highly spoken of by the English papers at the time. In 1861 he read papers before public meetings on the Manners and Customs of the Parsees and on the Parsee Religion. In the same year Mr. Dadabhai and other Parsees resident in London worked hard in the matter of Dr. Muncherjee Byramjee Colab, who was shut out from the competition for the Indian Medical Service. Dr. Muncherjee now occupies a high position in the service. In 1865 Mr. Dadabhai addressed the London Indian Society on the subject of the rules for the Civil Service examinations; and the discussion at and the representations made by the Society to the then Secretary of State for India succeeded in getting the marks for Sanskrit and Arabic restored to the former

figures which they had been reduced. In 1866 Mr.
Dadabhai read a paper before the Ethnological Society on
'The European and Asiatic Races,' with a view to vindi-
cate the character of the latter from the attack and asper-
sions made by Mr. Crawford, the president of the Society.
The rest of Mr. Dadabhai's disinterested labours were
confined mostly to the papers he read before the East
India Association, and to the part he took in the discussion
of papers read before the Association by other gentlemen.
The papers he read in the year 1867 were on—England's
Duties to India; Mysore; Memorial and Address for the
Admission of Natives into the Indian Civil Service; and
the expenses of the Abyssinian War. The papers read
in 1868 were—Memorial of the Natives of the Bombay
Presidency resident in England and correspondence with
Sir Stafford Northcote for the establishment of Female
Normal Schools as proposed by Miss Carpenter; Admission
of educated Natives into the Indian Civil Service; Reply
to Sir Stafford Northcote's speech in Parliament on the
subject; Correspondence with Sir Stafford Northcote on
the Indian Civil Service clause in the Governor-General of
India Bill; Reply to Lord William Hay on Mysore; Duties
of Local Indian Associations, and Irrigation Works in
India. We need scarcely say that since 1866 Mr. Dadabhai is better known for his work in connection with the
East India Association and the championship of the right
of the Indian people. On his return to Bombay in 1869
for a time, the native community of Bombay voted him an
address, a purse, and a portrait. Out of this purse, he
has, according to general report, spent the greater portion
in works of public usefulness. By far his most important
and earnest labour has for some years past been directed
to an exposition of the poverty of India and its remedy;
and anybody who carefully reads his papers on the subject,
read before the Bombay Branch of the East India Association, will see how thoroughly and earnestly he has discussed the subject. Latterly he has carried on some
direct correspondence on this subject with the India Office,
with some good effect; and has succeeded in awakening
an intelligent and sympathising interest in England in
connection with this matter. With respect to Mr. Dadabhai's public labours since 1868, we may say that in 1869
he delivered three Gujeratee and one English lecture for
the East India Association, and an address at the form-

ation and inauguration of the Bombay Branch. About the
same time he delivered a lecture in Gujeratee on ' The
Condition of India' at a meeting called by the Thakore
Saheb of Gondal; wrote another paper on the Civil Service
clause in the Governor-General of India Bill, which was
sent from Bombay to the East India Association ; and one
on the Bombay Cotton Act of 1869, which, with the discussions on the subject, resulted in the Act being vetoed by
the Secretary of State. In 1870 he wrote a paper on the
Wants and Means of India ; and in 1871 on the Commerce
of India, and on the Financial Administration of India.
In 1872, while in Bombay, he took an active part in the
agitation for municipal reform. In 1872 Mr. Dadabhai
gave evidence before the Parliamentary Select Committee.
In 1874 he entered on the duties of the Dewanship of
Baroda at the earnest solicitation of the Gaekwar, being
the first Parsee Dewan in an important Native State at a
time when the administration of its affairs was beset with
serious and harassing difficulties. His views, theoretical
and practical, of governings were truth and straightforwardness ; that governments and princes were made for
the people, and not the people for them ; and that the true
welfare of a State was identified with the welfare and
progress of the people. The space at our command pre-
cludes us from referring to the crowding incidents of that
year, and we must refer our readers to Mr. Dadabhai's
reply to the Baroda Blue-books. It may be remarked that
the struggle, in which a Resident was removed by a Viceroy
like Lord Northbrook, must have been one of no ordinary
character. The removal of a Resident for the sake of a
native Dewan is an event of rare occurrence. Sir Bartle
Frere, writing to Mr. Dadabhai in February 1874, said :—
' I have received with the utmost interest all the information you have sent home regarding your doings at Baroda.
You must not be discouraged by anything that happens.
You have undertaken, as I warned you, a terrible difficult
work, but I feel sure you have undertaken it in the right
spirit, and from none but the purest motives.' Again in
the following year Sir Bartle Frere wrote to Mr. Dadabhai :
' It has been a matter of regret to both of us (himself and
Sir Erskine Perry) that you were not allowed an opportunity of carrying out the reforms you desired, and thus
making one of the most interesting experiments possible
in a Native State. But you have the consolation of having

done your best. I do not see that any human being could have done more under the circumstances.' In 1875, during his stay in Bombay, Mr. Dadabhai was elected a member of the Corporation and of the Town Council, and worked in those offices for a little over a year. His treatment of some of the more troublesome questions of several years' standing elicited from the Corporation a special vote of thanks for his 'zeal and ability,' and an expression of regret at his resignation in September 1876. In addition to the routine work, his principal work during the year was showing that Government were demanding from the Municipality fifty lakhs of rupees more than they were entitled to on the Vehar Loan, and that the delivery of water by the Vehar system was only about fourteen gallons a head per day, and not seventeen gallons; and suggestions for loans for improvements and for amendments in the Municipal Act. In 1876 Mr. Dadabhai wrote his two papers on 'The Poverty of India,' which were read before the Bombay Branch of the East India Association; and his reply to the discussion on the poverty of India. From 1876 to 1879 he carried on a private correspondence with Sir Erskine Perry on the higher and larger employment of natives, and with Sir David Wedderburn about getting return of the salaries, pensions, &c., given to European employés in all departments of the State. In 1880 he wrote letters to the Secretary of State on the Productions and Wants of the Punjaub and India; a letter to the same high authority on 'The Moral Poverty of India and Native Thoughts on the present British Indian Policy,' and 'A few statements in the Report of the Finance Commission of 1880.' From 1878 to 1881 Mr. Dadabhai carried on a private correspondence with Mr. Hyndman on Indian subjects.

"Mr. Dadabhai was appointed a member of the Grand Jury in 1855; was nominated a Fellow of the Bombay University in 1864, and a Justice of the Peace in 1883, in which year he again joined the Corporation. Since his return to Bombay he has started the *Voice of India*. He submitted a note on education to the Education Commission when they held their sittings in Bombay. He made praiseworthy exertions for the success of the Ripon Memorial."

In August 1885, Lord Reay appointed Mr. Dadabhai an Additional Member of the Bombay Legislative Council.

2

His appointment was hailed with universal satisfaction, though it was felt by all that very tardy justice was done to him by Government. Mr. Dadabhai took a leading part at the meetings of the First Indian National Congress which sat in Bombay on the 27th, 28th and 29th December 1885. A few months after he left for England with a view to try his chance at the General Election and secure a seat in Parliament, the help of several English friends of India enabled him to find a constituency willing to accept him as a candidate. At a meeting of the Executive Committee of the Holborn Liberal Association, held on Friday, the 18th of June 1886, it was unanimously resolved to commend him to the Electors of Holborn as " a fit and proper person to represent the Liberals and Radicals of the Borough in Parliament." Mr. Dadabhai accepted the candidature and issued his address to the Electors of the Holborn Division of Finsbury on the 19th of June 1886. The issue at the General Elections of June 1886 turned upon the question of Home Rule for Ireland, and the English public were so much divided in opinion on the question, and besides, so strongly Conservative was the borough selected by Mr. Dadabhai, that from the first the chances of his election seemed slender. Most things were against him in the contest, but nevertheless he threw himself into it with great courage and resolution. He addressed a large number of meetings and was at all of them received most enthusiastically. Many of the English papers noticed his candidature and spoke favorably of the impression he had in a few days succeeded in making on the mind of his audiences. Mr. Dadabhai was defeated at the elections, he securing 1,950 votes while his Conservative opponent secured 3,651. Mr. Dadabhai's defeat was, under the circumstances, a victory. When he accepted the candidature, it was feared that he would hardly be able to secure 500 votes. The constituency was known to be strongly Conservative, and Mr. Dadabhai's opponent, Col. Duncan, had almost everything on his side—wealth, local influence, and the English antipathy to Mr. Gladstone's Home Rule policy for Ireland. That fighting against such odds, Mr. Dadabhai should have been able to secure so many as 1,950 votes, surprised all who had feared that he might not be able to secure even half that number. While in England he wrote in the *Times* and *Daily News* several letters on Exchange and

Bi-Metallism, then the most pressing of Indian economical questions. Mr. Dadabhai returned to India in November with a view to join the second Indian National Congress which was to assemble in Calcutta in the closing days of December. He was elected President of the Congress, and the address he delivered at the opening of it in the large hall of the Calcutta Town Hall is notable for the moderation of its tone, and the spirit of loyalty and reform which breathed through it.

II.

Mr. Dadabhai Naoroji's Election Address.

The following is the text of Mr. Dadabhai Naoroji's election address to the electors of Central Finsbury, Clerkenwell :—

To the Electors of Central Finsbury, Clerkenwell.

Gentlemen and Fellow Electors,—I have the honor to solicit votes at the next Parliamentary General Election, trusting that you will elect me to the House of Commons as your representative. I have been a resident and taxpayer in England connected with our Borough for the last four years. Should you do me the honor to return me, I will devote all my time to Parliamentary duties, and your local wants and interests shall have my especial attention. Events of the past week have happily left me the sole Liberal and Radical claimant to your consideration. I have the united support of all the Liberal and Radical organisations in Central Finsbury, and of the leading Liberal Party organisations ; I am, therefore, encouraged to hope that your votes, aided by their efforts made on my behalf, will be successful in returning me by a large majority to the House of Commons. For this amalgamation, and the kindly personal consideration I have always received from you, I return my sincere acknowledgments. My views on English politics are well known to you. These views I need not detail here, as many opportunities will be afforded at the public meetings, where I shall have the honor and pleasure to address you. I adopt the entire Newcastle tiberal programme, and give some of the principal measures Lherein contained, as well as others which I think are required : Home Rule for Ireland ; Home Rule for London ;

Endowment of the London County Council with full municipal powers, including the control of the police, water, gas or electric light supplies, public markets, trams, docks, hospitals, open spaces, and all other municipal necessities, with suitable housing for the people; effective compulsion upon owners to place their property in an habitable and sanitary condition; proper application of charitable endowments for the benefits of the people; women to be qualified for seats in the County Council; contribution by owners of property for public permanent improvements; rating of vacant property of land; representative parish and district councils; no rating qualifications for their members, and their election expenses to be paid from the rates; compulsory powers to local authorities to acquire and hold land for public purposes; education free, efficient, and under public control; triennial Parliaments; abolition of the hereditary principle in legislation; a simple system of registration of voters by responsible public registration officers: one man one vote only; one vote one value and power: one and the same day for all Parliamentary and Municipal Election; one register for all elections; payment by the State to returning officers and to members of the County Council and the Members of the House of Commons; all London to be one registration area for successive occupation, and a second ballot; taxation of ground rents and land values for Municipal and national purposes; division of rates between owners and occupiers; equalisation of rates, taxation of mining royaltes; direct popular veto of the liquor traffic; extension of the factory acts; free breakfast table; full compensation to tenants, whether of land or houses, for all improvements, good will or disturbance; a careful consideration of the right disposal of "unearned increment," a system of betterment, graduated income-tax on incomes above £300 a year, and higher rate on incomes derived by will, etc., on a sliding scale; also legal eight hours or forty-eight hours per week; payment of trade Union rates of wages in all public contracts; inexpensive industrial courts, generally all labor questions with a view to justice and fair play to labor; Indian reforms. Trusting that you will do me the honor to return me to Parliament as your representative, and again thanking you for your many kindnesses to me,—I have the honor to be, yours faithfully,

D. NAOROJI.

Accompanying the address were a number of " commendatory " letters from Mr. Gladstone; Miss Florence Nightingale ; Sir Charles Russell ; the Marquis of Ripon ; the Earl of Rosebery ; the Earl of Aberdeen ; Sir John Budd Phear and Captain Luthell, Candidates for Devonshire Divisions ; Mrs. " Josephine " Butler; Mr. Richard Eve, M.P. ; G. J. Holyoake. Esq. ; Dr. Pankhurst ; Mr. Edward Johnson (of Johnson Brothers, late Member for Exeter) ; Mrs. McLaren ; Mr. R. V. Barrow, Candidate for Bermonnrey; Mr. James Rowlands, M.P. ; Mr. George Bateman, Candidate for Holborn ; Mr. W. Dunn ; Candidate for Exeter ; Mr. John Coles ; Miss Colenso ; the Rev. Chaplin ; the Rev. J. S. Jones ; Mr. Sydney Stern, M.P. ; and Lord Reay, who wrote : " Dear Mr. Naoroji,—Your admission to the House of Commons would be welcomed by all those who are interested in the welfare of this Empire. You would speak with knowledge and experience on Indian questions, as well as on trade questions generally. As a member of the Legislative Council of Bombay, you have displayed talents which could not fail to be appreciated in the House of Commons. With my best wishes for your success,—I am, yours faithfully,

REAY.

III.

Scene at the Hustings.

(FROM THE LONDON LETTER TO *The Bombay Gazette.*)

Whatever may be said respecting the mixed feeling with which certain wire-pullers must have received the news of Mr. Dadabhai Naoroji's election by the narrow majority of three—they are accustomed to narrow majorities in Central Finsbury—there is no doubt about the popularity of the victory among the masses. Mr. Dadabhai ever since his appearance in the political arena has paid assiduous court to the horny-handed sons of toil ; has closely studied what is called the social problem ; and has never refused to impart the results of his investigations to those whose want of leisure prevents them looking very closely into such matters themselves. There is, I should imagine, hardly a working men's Radical Club in the

Metropolis at which he has not lectured during the past five or six years. At the Embankment "temple of luxury and ease," now a temple of excitement and bustle, elaborate arrangements both inside and outside have been made for recording the results of the contests immediately they are arrived at. Every evening a closely-packed crowd fills the space between the Hotel Metropole and the Charing Cross Railway Bridge to read the returns shown by magic lantern on a white screen erected on the Club's capacious terrace. On Wednesday night, before the actual figures were received, it was known that Mr. Dadabhai had been returned. The news spread to the multitude below, and soon there were heard shouts of "Three cheers for Salisbury's black man." The people in the street not knowing that a fresh count had been demanded in the interest of Captain Penton became impatient and angrily called for the Finsbury numbers. If the newly-made Parsee M.P. had been present, he could not have helped being gratified at the good-will shown to him by this concourse of Londoners; but he might possibly have thought some of his impetuous friends slightly wanting in respect. "Put the black man up" was frequently shouted out. "Up with the Day and Martin" was another exclamation. Much amusement was created by some one inquiring "Can't you write his name?" When at last the corrected figures showing that in spite of the stupendous obstacles with which he has had to contend, the plucky and determined stranger had beaten the powerful, local landlord, the enthusiasm was unmeasured. The cheering might almost have been heard at St. Paul's on one side and Chelsea Hospital on the other. At this time intelligence of Liberal successes was arriving pretty fast, and information of Gladstonian reverses had not yet come to cool the ardour of the zealots; accordingly they were in a frantic state of joy and gave vent to their exalted glee not only by the ordinary applause, but by singing a political version of "Ta-ra-ra boom-de-ay" as well as the illustrious chevaliers equally admired an elegant composition "Knocked 'em in the old Kent Road." Another section of the throng, and not a small one, exhibited its revolutionary tendencies by rendering in unison the "Marseillaise" à la Miss (or is it Mrs?) Shaw *labelle siffleuse*. Mr. Dadabhai did not put in an appearance at the Liberal Club the same night, but he was there yesterday evening and received what is called an ovation from his fellow Liberals. An eye-witness thus records the scene :— " Central Finsbury's Naoroji was dragged triumphantly to the platform and compelled to give a little speech. With a quiet grace which it is hoped will yet some day bring the blush of shame to Lord Salisbury "—poor Lord Salisbury, how he is made to suffer for his *lapsus linguæ!*—" he thanked the members of the Club for their uniform kindness to him during six years' membership, and while bespeaking a continued support in the consideration he would give to Indian questions, he assured his constituents that having all his time at his command he would be able to do them full justice." As might be expected, the Indian colony in London is delighted that one of their members should have succeeded in fighting his way to the proud position of an M.P. A respected co-religionist of Mr. Dadabhai and an old resident in this country has shown his gratitude to the Finsburyites by sending to the Lord Mayor the sum of one hundred guineas as a contribution to the Mansion House poor-box.

The Result of the Polling.

Hon. D. Naoroji	...	...	... 2,959
Captain F. T. Penton	...	...	... 2,956
			3

It is gratifying to know that Mrs. Bradlaugh-Bonner worked hard and heartily for Mr. Naoroji. Among other services which she rendered his candidature was the addressing of two meetings, one in the open-air, the other under cover. Mr. Naoroji had much help from the outside on the day of polling : among others, H. H. the Gaekwar of Baroda sent carriages to help to bring voters to the polling-booth.

Mr. Naoroji's Letter of Thanks to his Electors.

"National Liberal Club, Whitehall Place, S. W., 7th July, 1892.

"DEAR SIR,—I desire to take the earliest possible opportunity of tendering to all the electors of Central Finsbury my most grateful thanks for the honor they

have conferred on me by placing me in the proud position
of Parliamentary Representative for Central Finsbury.

"I also desire to offer my deep acknowledgments to all
who have aided me in my work at much self-sacrifice and
trouble. Having had so much voluntary assistance from
many quarters, it would be impossible for me to thank each
individually. I pray, therefore, every one to accept my
heartfelt thanks.

"When I first came among you, more than four years
ago, I promised that, if elected, the interests of Clerkenwell will always receive my first and principal consideration.
That promise shall be by me faithfully performed, as well
as all the pledges in my programme, and I trust your
entire satisfaction.

"You have in electing me generously and nobly helped
India to obtain a voice in the Imperial Parliament, and
I offer to you, on behalf of my countrymen, our most
sincere and heartfeltt hanks."—l remain, ever faithfully
yours,

D. NAOROJI.

IV.

The Scrutiny.

(FROM THE LONDON LETTER TO *The Bombay Gazette*.)

The words scrutiny and petition as applied to Finsbury,
writes a contributor to the local paper, are very old
acquaintances. I do not know how often they were used
here before my time, but most certainly they have been
revived at every Parliamentary election ever since I can
remember an election here at all, and that is now over
forty years ago. Alderman Challis, Remington Mills,
Major Reed, Lieut. Gill, William Cox, Dr. Perfitt, Sergeant
Parry, besides others I could name, were all either going
to bring petitions or scrutinies, or else have petitions and
scrutinies against them, but dear me, never one of them
has come off yet, and on search being made for the authors
of these "certain facts" people, well something else had
cropped up which took the bloom off, and we heard no

more about it, except from the people who never went through the process of brassing up.

Up to the present time no petition for scrutiny has been lodged, and the persons to whom communication of it must first be made know nothing at all about it. Mr. Penton last time won by five votes, and smiled for six years. Now after a bigger fight he lost by three; some of his misguided friends appear to go on with a parrot cry, and want very foolishly to put their champion to about two thousand pounds expense to find out how each of the objected people voted. A scrutiny is, my friends, a two-edged sword which cannot be played with with impunity, as it cuts more ways than one; fortunately they are very rare events, and according to what I can read it is better to accept defeat with good submissive grace, rather than stir up the strife which will be a natural outcome. If Mr. Penton's friends are loyal to him they should drop all talk of a scrutiny, which looks very much like putting the defeated candidate in a much greater minority. I know certain facts as well as Mr. Penton, and shall use them if the time ever comes. Mr. Naoroji and his friends have no fear.

Last Friday night, a few hours after the mail closed, Mr. Dadabhai Naoroji, M.P., received the unwelcome intelligence that Captain Penton intended to demand a recount and scrutiny. The information reached Mr. Dadabhai in the form of a letter from a firm of lawyers, who asked him to name some one on whom the petition could be served, or to say when it would be convenient for him to personally receive it. After consulting his friends Mr. Dadabhai placed the matter in the hands of Mr. Henry Cobb, of Lincoln's Inn Fields, who, as the son of a well-known Liberal M.P., is well up in election business. Up to Thursday afternoon Mr. Dadabhai had not seen the petition, but according to a paragraph that has appeared in the *Standard*, it charges not only personation but illegal practices and employment. But it is customary to make these allegations which may mean much or nothing. Some people think that Captain Penton will not go on with the case, but I cannot share their opinion, although it is whispered that certain influences are being exercised to induce the defeated candidate to withdraw his petition and take his beating gracefully. It is argued by some of Mr. Dadabhai's friends that Captain Penton having himself sat as M.P. for Central Finsbury with a majority of only five votes ought certainly to leave his opponent in undisturbed possession until the next General Election comes round. The gallant officer would, however, probably reply that in politics everything is fair, and from his point of view he is perfectly justified in unseating Mr. Dadabhai if he can. The Captain has deposited the sum of £1,000 in court as required by law, and it looks as if he meant business. The result of the Greenock petition being in favor of Sir Thomas Sutherland will probably encourage the Conservative to go on.

The native community of Bombay will rejoice at the gratifying result of the official recount of the votes in Central Finsbury, which raises Mr. Dadabhai Naoroji's majority of three to five—the precise number which sufficed to give Captain Penton nearly six years of Parliamentary life. The petition for a scrutiny is now withdrawn; but the result, so far as it went, improves the status of the sitting member by nearly doubling his majority. A scrutiny pushed, as Mr. Goschen would say to the bitter end, is a tedious and costly operation, and there is seldom much to justify the expectation that the votes invalidated, if any, would be all on one side. Since the introduction of voting by ballot, it is only when a scrutiny is demanded that the papers once sealed and put away can be re-opened. In a rigid scrutiny every voting paper is compared with the official register and the validity of each vote tendered is put to the test. There was another course open to Captain Penton, similar to that which the Liberals of East Manchester propose to adopt against Mr. Balfour's return. They might have preferred the claim to the seat before the judges appointed to deal with election petitions. The allegations on which they based their claim would be investigated, and their lordships would then decide and report to the speaker which candidate has been elected. When corrupt practices have been proved, the judges report whether the candidate was cognizant of them. When such a report is made, a Royal Commission is appointed, and this decides whether or not it is desirable to issue a fresh writ or hold it in abeyance, leaving the

constituency for a time unrepresented. We do not suppose Captain Penton had any grounds for imputing corrupt practices, or he would not have been slow to state
them. By Mr. Dadabhai Naoroji's many friends in India
it was feared that the result of the scrutiny in Central
Finsbury would prove similar to that at Greenock, where
Sir Thomas Sutherland took the place of Mr. Bruce, who
was at first officially declared to be elected. This appre-
hension is now dissipated.—*Bombay Gazette.*

A petition has, however, been presented. The following
is the full text of the petition that has been presented to
the High Court of Justice, Queen's Bench Division, by
Captain Penton, who describes himself as of Chalfont
Park, near Slough, in the county of Buckingham. The
petition, which was filed on the 26th ultimo, was as follows.
The result of the petition is being awaited by the Indian
people with considerable anxiety :—

1. Your petitioner was a candidate, and claims to have
had a right to be returned at the above election.

2. Your petitioner states that the election was holden
on the 6th day of July in the year of our Lord, 1892,
when your petitioner and Dadabhai Naoroji were candidates, and the Returning Officer has returned the said
Dadabhai Naoroji as being duly elected.

3. And your petitioner says that mistakes were made
by the Returning Officer, his assistants, and clerks in the
counting of the votes, and that by reason of such mistakes
the result of the poll was not truly ascertained.

4. That certain persons whose names appear on the
Register of Voters of the said division voted twice at the
said election in favour of the said 'Dadabhai Naoroji, or
voted first in other divisions of the said borough, and
subsequently again in favour of the said Dadabhai Naoroji.

5. That certain persons personated and voted as and
for certain other persons, whose names appear on the
Register of Voters of the said division as electors, some of
whom also voted, and some of whom were dead, and some
of whom did not themselves vote.

6. That certain votes given at the said election for
Dadabhai Naoroji were given upon ballot papers not duly

marked with the official mark, or which had thereon writings or marks by which the voter could be identified, or which were unmarked or void for uncertainty, and that such votes or some of them were erroneously received as good votes, and were counted for the said Dadabhai Naoroji.

7. That certain persons voted at the said election and were reckoned upon the poll for the said Dadabhai Naoroji, who were before, at, and after the said election, guilty of bribery, cheating, and undue influence, and other corrupt and illegal practices.

8. That certain persons voted at the said election and were reckoned upon the poll for the said Dadabhai Naoroji, who were bribed, threatened, and unduly influenced to vote thereat for Dadabhai Naoroji.

9. That certain persons voted at the said election and were reckoned upon the poll for the said Dadabhai Naoroji, who were and had been disqualified by legal incapacity to vote, and who were prohibited by law from voting by virtue of divers statutes or by the common law of Parliament.

10. That certain persons voted and were reckoned upon the poll for the said Dadabhai Naoroji, who were disqualified to vote at the said election by reason of their holding or having held disqualifying offices or employment or having been retained, hired, or employed for reward for the purposes of the said election as agents, clerks, messengers, or otherwise.

11. That the votes of all the aforesaid persons were wholly null and void, and ought to be struck off the poll of the said Dadabhai Naoroji.

12. That the majority of the votes declared by the Returning Officer in favour of the said Dadabhai Naoroji was only an apparent and colourable majority, and that the real majority of good and legal votes polled at the said election was in favor of your petitioner.

13. That the said Dadabhai Naoroji, by himself and his election agent, was guilty of illegal payments, illegal employment and illegal hirings before, during, and after the said election.

14. That the said Dadabhai Naoroji by himself and

his election agent before, during and after the said
election, and for the purpose of promoting or proving the
election of the said Dadabhai Naoroji, engaged and employed persons for payment or promise of payment for
purposes and incapacities other than those allowed by law.

15. That the said Dadabhai, by himself and his agents
and by other persons on his behalf before, during, and
after the said election knowingly made payments and
contracts, for payments to and with electors on account
of the use of houses, buildings, or premises for the exhibition of addresses, bills, and notices and on account of the
exhibition of addresses, bills, and notices.

16. That the said Dadabhai Naoroji, by himself and
his agents and other persons on his behalf before, during,
and after the said election knowingly made payments and
contracts for payments on account of the conveyance of
voters to and from the poll, and were guilty of illegal
hirings in contravention of Section 14 of the said Act.

17. That the said Dadabhai Naoroji, by himself and his
agents and other persons on his behalf before, during, and
after the said election made payments in respect of expenses incurred on account of and in respect of the conduct
and management of the said election otherwise than by or
through the Election Agent of the said Dadabhai Naoroji.

18. That the said Dadabhai Naoroji, by himself and
his election agent before, during, and after the said election knowingly provided money for payments and expenses
and for replacing money expended in payments and expenses, and knowingly paid sums and incurred expenses
on account of and in respect of the conduct and management of the said election in excess of the maximum
amounts in that behalf respectively specified in the
Schedule of the Act 46 and 47 Victoria, Ch. 51, and in
contravention of the said Act.

19. And your petitioner says that by reason of matters
herein set forth, the said Dadabhai Naoroji was and is in-
capacitated from serving in the present Parliament for the
said division of the said borough, and that the said election
and the said return of the said Dadabhai Naoroji were and
are wholly null and void.

20. Wherefore your petitioner prays, that it may be
ordered that the ballot papers be recounted so that the

correct numbers assuming to vote for each candidate may be ascertained, and that it may be determined that the said Dadabhai Naoroji was not duly elected, and that the said election and return of the said Dadabhai Naoroji were and are wholly null and void, and that your petitioner was duly elected and ought to have been returned to serve as a member for the said division of the said borough in this present Parliament.

V.

Congratulations in India.

1. Public Meeting at Bombay.

(*The Bombay Gazette.*)

The Bombay Town Hall has certainly never held within its walls a larger or more enthusiastic gathering than that which assembled on Saturday afternoon, to rejoice over the election of Mr. Dadabhai Naoroji and return their heartfelt thanks to the electors of Central Finsbury for voting for him. An hour before the advertised time of the demonstration the hall was packed to its utmost limit, and there was not a place vacant from where the platform could be seen, or the speeches could be heard.

Hundreds of people failed to gain admittance, and when Sir Dinshaw Manockji Petit took the chair, there must have been over two thousand persons in the hall. These represented every section of the community, and all evinced the greatest enthusiasm in the proceedings, listening attentively to the speeches, and cheering the speakers to the echo.

On the motion of Mr. Verjeevandas Mahadhowdas, seconded by Mr. Sorabjee Framjee Patel, Sir Dinshaw Manockjee Petit, Bart., was called to the chair.

The Chairman, who was enthusiastically received, said : Gentlemen,—We have met here, as you are all aware, to give expression to the extreme gratification which we all feel at the election for the first time of a Native of India to a seat in the British Parliament. The merit of the cause which has occasioned this large gathering representative of the different races and interests of this great City commends itself so well that I shall not detain you by any lengthy remarks of mine in justification of our assembling here to-day. View the affair from whatever point you like, the election of Mr. Dadabhai Naoroji to a seat in the Imperial Parliament is an event fraught with consequences beneficial and important to India. (Loud cheers.) The edifying spectacle presented by the Electors of Finsbury of returning to Parliament as their representative a gentleman alien to them in race, creed and religion tends to strengthen our conviction as regards high-mindedness and sense of fair play characteristic of Englishmen. (Loud cheers.) The gentleman who has won for himself this high honor is by common consent the one Native of India who by his character, varied attainments and long experience of public life, best fitted to shine in that august assembly. The perseverance and zeal which struggled so long and against such odds deserved success which has not been long in coming. (Loud and prolonged cheers.) With these few remarks, gentlemen, I call upon Mr. P. M. Mehta to propose his resolution.

Mr. P. M. Mehta, who was received with loud and prolonged cheers, said :—

Mr. Chairman and Gentlemen,—We are met to-day to give as it were a formal welcome to those "glad tidings of great joy" of the election of a Native of India—(cheers) and that native, Mr. Dadabhai Naorojee (renewed cheers,—as a member of Parliament which have rejoiced, I think I may say it without exaggeration, the heart of every man, woman and child throughout the length and breadth of this land. I do not know, gentlemen, if you are aware how entirely appropriate it is that a public meeting for this object should be convened by the Bombay Presidency Association. (Cheers.) I do not know if you remember that the struggle which Mr. Dadabhai has brought to so successful and glorious a termination, and in which he has proved that he is made of the stuff of which heroes are made, is a veritable Seven Years' War, the opening campaign of which had for its scene of operations and battle-field this City of Bombay and the rooms of the Association. (Cheers.) Much about this time seven years ago, at the time when the General Elections of 1885 was pending, the Association resolved to inaugurate the policy of carrying the war as it were into the enemy's

country, of making a direct appeal to the British electors
by means of leaflets and delegates, and of asking them to
discriminate between the white sheep and the black sheep
among those who offered themselves for election as the
friends of Indians, and the representatives of their
interests, for it is a remarkable fact, gentlemen, that Anglo-
Indians, the most perverse, never tire of posing as our only
genuine friends and the sole repositories of our confidence
and our affections. (Laughter.) It is a curious coincidence
that at the meeting held for this purpose, we had the same
chairman, who so worthily presides to-day, then Mr. (now
Sir) Dinshaw Petit—(cheers —but then, as now, always
ready and willing to lend a helping hand to every just and
true cause. Many of those who took part in that day's
proceedings have since risen to distinction, the first resolution being moved by the Hon'ble Mr. Justice Telang,
whose elevation to the Bench would be a source of the
most unalloyed gratification, if it did not leave his friends
on many an important occasion without the aid of his
sound and sympathetic judgment, his temperate and
judicious guidance, his cultured and thoughtful eloquence.
(Applause.) I shall never cease to regret the untimely death
of another speaker at the meeting, my late lamented friend
Mr. Dinsha Kanga, who had given high promise of a
career of great public usefulness. One of the best pieces
of work we did on that occasion was that we discovered
my friend Mr. Chandavarkar (cheers)—whom we packed
off straight to England, where, I need not tell you, how
greatly he distinguished himself. But of those who
took part in the proceedings of that day, there was nobody
who threw himself into the movement inaugurated by the
Association more earnestly or more vigorously than
Mr. Dadabhai. He had only a short while before emerged
from that seclusion into which the black outlook on the
political horizon in Lord Lytton's time had driven him in
despair and disappointment. I do not think it is generally
known that it is to Lord Ripon—(loud cheers)—among
our other numerous debts that we owe the return of
Mr. Dadabhai to public life, just as we now owe his Lordship our grateful acknowledgments for the sympathy and
support uniformly extended by him by speeches and letters,
as you must have seen from the English papers, throughout the whole of Mr. Dadabhai's candidature. (Cheers.)
Animated by a new hope and a new spirit which Lord

Ripon's Viceroyalty awakened in him, Mr. Dadabhai soon set to work again with the same unselfish devotion and the same untiring energy which have always honourably distinguished his public career. It was he who moved the principal resolution at the meeting, and struck the keynote of the situation by emphatically laying down that "it is in Parliament our chief battles have to be fought." To this he soon came to add another article of faith to his political creed, in favor of which I had ventured to raise my solitary voice at the meeting. It was that not only our chief battles have to be fought in Parliament, but that those battles could never be really or truly fought until Indian questions were brought within the sphere of party politics. I am ready to admit, gentlemen, that there is no sophistry more plausible than that which advises us to behave like the donkey in the fable stuck between two panniers of hay, both of them supposed to be equally good and equally delicious. (Laughter.) But believe me, gentlemen, there is no sophistry more pernicious or more opposed to our real interests. While England is governed as it is by the machinery of party, there is no salvation for us until Indian questions are sifted in the fierce light of party contention. His Excellency the Governor—(cheers)—was so far quite right the other day, when he said that we could never know the utmost that could be said on either side of a question until the interested zeal of a party press was brought to bear upon it. To take only one instance, do you think, gentlemen, there is only hope for us to be saved from that disastrous military policy, and that frightful military expenditure wickedly draining the resources of the country, which would otherwise fructify and multiply a thousandfold in innumerable directions, until they are remorsely exposed and criticised in the unsparing conflict of party warfare. (Hear, hear.) So impressed was Mr. Dadabhai with the force of these two political convictions that when the elections of 1885 went against our hopes and wishes, when Mr. Lalmohun Ghose, to whom in justice must always belong the credit of making the first practicable breach in the stronghold,—(cheers)—was defeated at Debtford, nothing could restrain Mr. Dadabhai from taking the firm determination of throwing himself into the breach, and leading the forlorn hope himself. Neither age—he was sixty then—nor any considerations of mere prudence could keep him back. He

4

left for England early in 1886, and for seven long years
has he labored and striven in what I have ventured to
designate a veritable Seven Years' War, unappalled by
the coldness and opposition of friend and foe, undismayed
by repulses, reverses, and defeats, never losing heart, and
never betrayed into saying or doing aught which might
misbecome him as we know him.

"A selfless man and stainless gentleman."

(Applause.) And the reward which such indomitable
pluck, patience and fortitude so richly deserve has at
length come to him. He has accomplished the noblest
ambition of his heart, he has realized the most romantic
dream of his life, he has achieved a distinction prouder
and nobler than any which title or orders could bestow, a
distinction more enduring than monuments of brass or
marble, a distinction which will live in history—the distinction of being the first Native of India to enter the portals
of an assembly, than which neither ancient nor modern
history has anything greater or grander to show, the
portals of the British House of Commons. (Loud applause.)
We are told, gentlemen, that there is nothing very much
in all this, that we are only bustling in a little comedy of
much ado about nothing; the colour-blind *Pioneer* cannot
see a trace of romance in the appearance of Mr. Dadabhai
in Parliament. But you know, gentlemen, that there are
people to whom, as to Peter Bell,

> " A Primrose by a river brim,
> A yellow primrose was to him,
> And it was nothing more."

But it may be pardoned to us if nurtured in some of
the noblest traditions of English history, we allow ourselves for a moment to be carried away by sentiment, if
we venture to contemplate with some degree of emotion
and reverence the spectacle of a native of India entering
that very assembly in which in terms of immortal eloquence, Burke and Fox and Sheridan pleaded the cause
of righteousness in the Government of this country, where
Macaulay saw in dim but prophetic vision the dawn of
that day which may bring us our political enfranchisement,
where Bright and Fawcett and Bradlaugh raised their
voice for justice to millions of voiceless and alien people.
(Loud applause.) There may be spectacles more dazzling
to the eye, more gorgeous with pageantry, more attrac-

tive to grown-up children, like unto the Imperial
jingoism. But to those who have humbly learnt to recognize that the greatest events have but small beginnings,
the appearance of the simple unassuming little " Black
Man " in the hall of Parliament is pregnant with deep
cause for loyal and hopeful thankfulness. To them it is a
visible symbol, a practical proof of the vitality of that
policy of righteousness which, in spite of many drawbacks
and many backslidings, has still retained predominance
as the declared and guiding policy of the Crown in India.
Many people profess to be sceptical as to the patriotism
and political sagacity of the electors of Central Finsbury
—(cheers)—in choosing an Indian for their representative.
But I think you will agree with me, gentlemen, that they
have rendered a service of incalculable value, by proving
by their generous action, that the instincts of English
political wisdom are capable of triumphing over the direct
prejudices of caste, color, and creed. (Cheers.) Nothing
is more calculated to stimulate and strengthen our loyalty
and our contentment than to find that the theoretical
privileges which we are supposed to possess as Her
Majesty's subjects are capable of being reduced into
accomplished facts. It may be, gentlemen, that no great
immediate consequences can or will follow from Mr.
Dadabhai's election. I am quite prepared to admit that
he will not take the House by storm ; I am also quite
prepared to admit that he will not set the Thames on fire.
But we shall be quite content with what he may be modestly able to perform. Of one thing we are sure, that,
be it much, or be it little, he will perform it with unselfish
zeal and devotion—earning for himself our unstinted
respect, affection and admiration, for the great Queen
whom he will serve, the increasing loyalty of her Indian
subjects, and for the country whom he loves so well, the
fairest prospects of a gradual development of political
progress.

> " Broadening slowly down from precedent to precedent."

(Loud and continued cheers.)

Mr. Mehta concluded by moving the first resolution :
" That in offering Mr. Dadabhai Naoroji their most cordial
congratulations as the first Native of India ever elected
to sit in the British House of Commons, the inhabitants
of this city in public meeting assembled desire to give

expression to their boundless satisfaction at the success
which has crowned his unselfish and devoted exertions
for the welfare of his country, and which have earned for
him the respect, affection, and admiration of all people."
(Loud cheers.)

Mr. Javerilal Umiashunkar Yajnik, in seconding
the proposition, said :—

Gentlemen,—My friend, Mr. Mehta, has given you
the history of Mr. Dadabhai's candidature, and he has
given it so fully and eloquently that he has left very little
for me to say on that point. No doubt for Mr. Dadabhai
the struggle was far too arduous as the prize to be won
was far too tempting. It must be remembered at the same
time that Mr. Dadabhai's friends in India were never sanguine about his success. They knew the immense difficulties he had to contend against. They knew that an English
constituency was more likely to send an English representative to Parliament than an Indian candidate. They also
believed in the proverbial indifference of British Electors
to India and her people. Of this indifference they had a
most recent instance in the farce which was played out a
few weeks ago in connection with the presentation of the
Indian Budget to the House of Commons. (Hear, hear.)
Fancy, gentlemen, only three members of that august
body, except the Speaker and the Hon. Mr. Curzon, being
present to listen to the tale of the Under-Secretary of
State for India, touching the affairs of the two hundred
and sixty millions of Her Majesty's subjects in this country.
With such a lack of interest in India, well might Mr.
Dadabhai's friends here suppose that his efforts to woo
and win an English constituency were doomed to disappointment. And if any one of them had any doubts
about this, those doubts were dispelled by Mr. Dadabhai's
own account of his difficulties. It seems that these difficulties began to increase as the Elections drew nearer. In
this situation, gentlemen, you may conceive with what
degree of agreeable surprise and with what thrill of joy
the news wired by Reuter about Mr. Dadabhai's return to
Parliament was received in Bombay and India. (Cheers.)
As in many other cases so in this, gentlemen, it is the
unexpected that has happened. The people of India
rejoice to find that their impressions about the attitude of
British Elections have been falsified. They feel and we

feel that the 2,659 Liberal Electors of Central Finsbury who went to poll on the 7th July and made it possible for Mr. Dadabhai to succeed have earned our lasting gratitude, for in honouring Mr. Dadabhai with their confidence, the electors have honoured the whole of the Indian people. (Cheers.) That day, gentlemen—the 7th of July—we regard as the proudest day in the political history of India as well as the Parliamentary history of England, for the success of that day marks an epoch in the annals of British Rule in India. We feel that in dealing with Mr. Dadabhai, those truly Liberal Electors of Centeral Finsbury have given evidence of a breadth of sentiment, a freedom from prejudice, and a degree of political sagacity and wisdom which does them infinite credit and infinite honour. They have shown that Englishmen can often rise above insular prejudices, for, as Tennyson reminds us :—

> Not once or twice in our rough island story
> The path of duty was the way to glory.

(Cheers.) Gentlemen, the London *Times* told us the other day that the return of a Native of India to Parliament was an interesting and romantic event. No doubt the election of any other Indian gentleman to Parliament would have been an equally interesting and romantic event. In the case of Mr. Dadabhai, however, there is this matter for congratulation, and that is that he is a tried representative of the constituency. During the four years that he nursed the Central Finsbury constituency, he was able to make it plain to his English Electors—to friends as well as to opponents alike—that though an Indian in blood and colour, and though a "Black Man," he was every inch an Englishman in point of character, in pluck, and perseverance, and in courage and self-reliance. (Cheers.) He satisfied them that his English education and English association for the best thirty years of his life had made his sense of justice and fair play as keen as that of any Englishman of culture, and that anxious as he was to get a victory over his opponent in fair fight, his sense of honour would rebel from doing anything he considered dishonourable to himself or his country. In short, gentlemen, Mr. Dadabhai was serving his apprenticeship under a sense of the highest responsibility. It is these English traits of character in Mr. Dadabhai and their appreciation by ladies and gentlemen of the highest position in life in

England that have won for Mr. Dadabhai the esteem and confidence of his Finsbury Electors. They were satisfied that the interests of their constituency would be as safe in his hands as in that of any English representative. Add to this the fact that Mr. Dadabhai was a native of India and that as such he would be the natural mouth-piece in Parliament of the voiceless millions of India. If his presence would do nothing else, it would at least deter members from palming off unfounded statements on the House. It was these considerations which influenced the good Electors of Central Finsbury in helping Mr. Dadabhai. (Cheers.) One word more, and I have done. The telegraph which announced the return of Mr. Dadabhai also reported the defeat of Mr. Maclean at Oldham. (Hisses.) Far be it from me, gentlemen, to refer to this incident in a spirit of exultation. Mr. Maclean, it must be admitted, is a gentleman of unquestioned abilities and debating powers. My object in referring to him is to show that if Mr. Maclean had been as good as his word and had faithfully carried out the challenge which he was the first to throw before the people of India about years ago when he was returned for Oldham, he would at this mo-ment have earned for himself the sympathy of the whole Indian people. What was that challenge? That chal-lenge, as communicated by Mr. Maclean in his weekly letter to the *Bombay Gazette*, dated 27th November 1885, was to the effect that " The Natives of India will now have an opportunity of judging for themselves if the man whom the Bombay Presidency Association proscribed is really an enemy to the country in which he made his fortune and reputation." And now, gentlemen, what is the fact after the lapse of over six years? The fact is that by his attitude of uncompromising hostility to the interests of India generally, and specially in the matter of Indian Factory Legislation and in the discussion in Parliament on the Indian Councils Act Amendment Bill, Mr. Maclean has proved to the hilt that the prophecy which the Bombay Presidency Association ventured upon six years ago has turned out to be true, and that the challenge thrown out by him at the time was a vain and empty boast. (Loud hisses.) Gentlemen, whatever may be said of the people of India, one point in their national character which does them credit is most noteworthy, and that is that they knew who their friends and benefactors among the governing classes are, and they know how to be grateful to them. (Loud cheers.)

Mr. W. A. Chambers, in supporting the resolution, said :—

I think I have every excuse for addressing you from this platform to-day, and in taking part in your rejoicings because, two years ago, I was a voter in Central Finsbury. (Applause.) The last Political Association to which I was elected was upon the Council, or Committee of Mr. Dadabhai. I am sorry to see and, I think, you must all be sorry to see, so few Englishmen taking part in this rejoicing and sympathising with you to-day upon the return of a clever and good son of India. (Hear, hear. I ask you, however, not to appeal to the few, the small minority of Englishmen in India, but to appeal to the great and large heart of it in England. (Loud applause.) You have appealed on two or three occasions, and on the last, they have elected one of you to their House of Parliament. (Cheers.) As I entered this hall this afternoon, I was given a caricature of Mr. Dadabhai, and he was represented with a staff in his hand bearing the words "Patience and Perseverance." I say to the young men of India, not as a politician or sympathiser with you, that if there is one example of patience and perseverance you ought to emulate, it is the patience and perseverance of Mr. Dadabhai. (Loud applause.) For four long years, in spite of the coolness of the official Liberal Party—for you have nothing to hope from them—in spite of the opposition of a Radical newspaper, which should have been on his side, I mean the *Star*, he has conquered and won. (Cheers.) As he said to me three years ago "they think they can keep down the mild Hindoo, but I will teach them. I will stick to this constituency." (Renewed cheers.) I was told, when I left England, that I would find the people of India have no sympathy with aspirations for political improvement. This meeting, I say, is an answer to that, for if I have seen larger meetings, I have never seen one more enthusiastic. In conclusion, I will say that Mr. Dadabhai is a man you can honour, for whilst he is gentle and modest, he has a determination that is ready to grapple with any obstacle, and you have chosen a clever and good man. (Loud applause.)

The resolution was then carried by acclamation.

Mr. R. M. Sayani said :—

Mr. Chairman and Gentlemen,—I beg to propose "That the thanks of the meeting be conveyed to the Electors of Central Finsbury for their generous and high-minded action in electing Mr. Dadabhai Naoroji as their member in Parliament." The proposition I have just submitted to you does not require any lengthened or laboured pleading or any pleading at all on my part to induce you to accept it. The good Electors of Central Finsbury deserve our warmest thanks for the favour they have done us by electing one of our fellow-countrymen to the highest popular assembly in the world. (Cheers.) From amongst themselves or from the innumerable public men of Great Britain they could have easily chosen somebody who might have equally served their purpose. But they have gone out of their way, and chosen an Indian gentleman as their representative in the House of Commons, and in doing so, they have shown a magnanimous and liberal spirit which marks them as the most liberal constituency even of liberal Great Britain, and this magnanimity and liberality of theirs are deserving of our deepest gratitude. We, in India, who know the individual of their choice as we know ourselves, have, of course, every hope that our fellow-countryman who has had the good luck of being so elected will fully justify their choice and will serve them as fully and as efficiently as any they could have possibly chosen, but our thanks to them are not for that reason the less hearty and sincere, for they have in electing him placed in him magnanimous and generous confidence which has rendered our country deeply indebted to them. (Cheers.) Although therefore we are very much beholden to the good folks of Central Finsbury, I am not at all surprised that an English constituency should elect an Indian gentleman, for experience teaches us that the good people of England are always willing that all their fellow-subjects, in whatever part of the Empire living, and even foreigners becoming naturalised in England, should have the same rights and privileges as they themselves; and herein lies the key to the success with which Great Britian has acquired such a vast Empire, and the British have been able to produce such immense and flourishing colonies. (Loud cheers.) We all know that in no part of the British Empire is there one law for one set of the inhabitants and another for another set of the inhabitants. In the eye of the law the rulers and the ruled, the rich and the poor are all alike, or to use an oriental phraseology, the tiger and the lamb may all drink at the same fountain, unmolested and unreservedly. The people of England are a hard-headed but a fair-headed people, and any one having a just cause has but to conscientiously and persistently knock at their door, and in the end he is sure to obtain admission. I have spoken above of the people of England, and not of the Government of England, and my reason is that it is not the so-called Government nor even the Crown that governs England. It is the people of England that govern England, and it is a misnomer to call the Government of England as a limited monarchy. It is really and truly speaking a limited Republic. It is a common wealth where the people are the sovereign—their will is law—subject to constitutional limits. Good luck has brought us into contact with such a people, and we have every chance in keeping ourselves allied to them, of raising ourselves to their high level, and of enjoying peace, prosperity, and also power, provided we are true to ourselves. Referring to our worthy countryman, in whose honour we have met here this evening, I need not say that a gentleman of his ability, integrity, and perseverance was bound to succeed in the end. He has set to his countrymen an example of self-devotion, devotion to duty which, it is to be trusted, we shall all take to heart, and I have no doubt that his example will stir up many an Indian to follow his footsteps and contribute towards the moral resurrection of our country. (Cheers.) For differing as we may well do as to the advisability or otherwise of becoming Conservatives, or Liberals or Radicals, or taking sides with any other party we are all agreed on the desirability, nay, the utter necessity, of shaking off our apathy and lethargy, the two great curses of India, and of adopting habits of energy and perseverance, if we at all want to become and to be recognized as men as being worthy of the blessings which a merciful Providence has showered on us by creating us human beings as the lords of the creation. And I hope it will not be considered out of place here to exhort my co-religionists to shake off their invariable apathy, which has now become almost synonymous with their name, for, and I hope they will pardon me for saying so, if they do not avail themselves of the numerous advantages and blessings

5

which the benign British Government has placed within their reach, if they lose this opportunity, they will not only be doomed for ever to the wretched condition they are in, but they will also hinder the progress of this country, and deserve the severe censure of the other races inhabiting this vast land. If, however, they will avail themselves of this opportunity, shake off their apathy, and put their own shoulders to the wheel, and we with the other races of India, and especially our Parsee fellow-subjects, in honest, conscientious and persistent endeavours to improve themselves, we shall yet, notwithstanding evil prophecies of certain publicists, raise the crescent, not by achievements on battle fields, but in the no less glorious but still more permanent paths of civil victories, for it is well to remind them that if the resurrection of Islam is to be anywhere, it is to be in British India under the auspices of the British Government. (Loud cheers.)

Mr. N. G. Chandravarkar, who was cordially received, in seconding the resolution said :—

Mr. Chairman and Gentlemen,—No language can adequately express how deeply our hearts are moved by the feeling of gratitude to the electors of Central Finsbury, for electing Mr. Dadabhai Naoroji as their member in Parliament. That feeling can only be equalled by the unbounded enthusiasm by which you are all inspired on this occasion. (Cheers.) We have chosen the simple and unostentatious language of this resolution to express those feelings, because when the heart is full, the simplest language is the best to convey its feelings. We are grateful to the electors of Central Finsbury for the sake of each one of us, India's sake, and for England's sake. We are grateful to them for the sake of each one of us, because when we received the news of Mr. Dadabhai's election, each one of us felt as if each one of us had been elected M. P. (Laughter and cheers.) We are grateful to them for India's sake, because they have immortalized themselves by being the first amongst the British electors to confer upon a Native of India the high and unprecedented honour of a member of Parliament, and by that noble action they have as it were poured new life into this country. We are grateful to them for England's sake, because we are deeply interested in whatever heightens the glory and popularity of

English rule, and we feel that by the election of Mr. Dadabhai as their member in Parliament, the electors of
Central Finsbury have shown that Englishmen can lift
themselves above their insular prejudices, and rise
practically to those noble instincts of that true and
generous imperialism which history consecrates because
it alone can preserve the empire that has been gained—
(loud cheers)—not that bastard imperialism, which
mistakes self-aggrandisement for real power, and bases
all government on selfish instincts. (Hear, hear.) The
electors of Central Finsbury deserve every credit for
having practically vindicated England's true position as
the mistress of the Empire, over which the sun never sets.
(Cheers.) I may be asked, how is it that the resolution now
before us asks us to thank the electors of Central Finsbury
in general, when, as a matter of fact, we know that it is
only the Liberal electors of that constituency who supported
Mr. Dadabhai, and enabled him to become a member of
Parliament. It is true that the Liberal electors of Central
Finsbury deserve our most heartfelt gratitude, that it
is to them we owe the present occasion. They will live
long in our memories and in our grateful hearts. But
in the resolution we include the electors in general, because Mr. Dadabhai will represent them all in Parliament.
The resolution speaks of the action of the electors of
Central Finsbury as generous and high-minded. It may
possibly be urged that as the electors have elected Mr.
Dadabhai to represent their interests in Parliament and not
India's, there is no reason why their action should be described by us as generous and high-minded. But although
if the electors of Central Finsbury had elected Mr. Dadabhai merely or mainly to represent India in Parliament,
and not on their own account, they would have done a good
and noble thing, yet their action would have merely been
an act of kindness to India. In that case there would have
been no very high honour conferred upon either Mr. Dadabhai or India. On the other hand, by electing a Native
of India to the House of Commons for the purpose of
representing an English constituency and defending its
interests in Parliament, they have conferred a much higher
honour upon Mr. Dadabhai, and through him on this
country, than if they had elected him simply or principally
for India's sake. (Cheers.) And now look at the noble
result which this generous and high-minded action of the

electors of Central Finsbury is calculated to have on the future of England and India. They have by means of it extended to us, the Natives of India, the right hand of fellowship in a manner which I should say is above all human, above all Roman, praise. (Cheers.) They have made us feel and realise more than ever that the spirit of equality, justice, and fair play does after all and in reality form the most ennobling and living feature of the British constitution. They have shown that when in 1833 the British Parliament conveyed to India by means of one of its statutes the assurance that England in her dealings with India would not be actuated by any considerations of race and religion, that when again Her Majesty the Queen reiterated that assurance in her noble proclamation of 1858, Her Majesty and the Parliament held out to this country no mere vain hope. That noble assurance of Her Majesty and of the Parliament the electors of Central Finsbury have emphasized by giving effect to it in the most noble manner they could. They have by their action drawn closer the ties by which England and India are held together. They have struck deeper into the soil of India the roots of British rule, struck deeper into our hearts the roots of our royalty to the government we live under. (Loud cheers.) They have not only made us feel and realize more than ever that England and India are one concern, that their interests are identical, that united they both stand, and divided they both fall; but they have also made us feel and realise that it is a proud privilege to be the subjects of Her Most Gracious Majesty the Queen of England and Empress of India. (Loud cheers.) They have brought home to our mind most forcibly the living force and truth of what the poet said when he spoke of England as

" A land of settled government,
A land of just and old renown,
Where freedom slowly broadens down
From precedent to precedent."

This is no mere rhetorical flourish or a mere ebullition of frothy sentiment, but a real fact, and in support of what I have now described to you as the noble result which the action of the electors of Central Finsbury is sure to produce on the future of British rule in India, I am content to appeal to the judgment seat and the verdict of history— that history, the lessons of which form the guiding principles of all true and sagacious statesmen. It must be a matter of pride and pleasure to us that the two English dailies of this city—the *Times of India* and the *Bombay Gazette*—have shown the fine and generous instinct of the Englishman in receiving with pleasure the news of Mr. Dadabhai's election. (Hear, hear. It is also gratifying to note that our Governor, H. E. Lord Harris, has, by gracefully and readily permitting the use of this Hall for this meeting, shown that he, as the representative of Her Majesty, is proud of our pride—the pride that has enabled us to meet to-day to proclaim the triumph of the British constitution, and of the British rule in India. (Hear, hear, and cheers.) The only discordant voice so far has come from Allahabad, the oracle of which has declared in his usual way that the British elector has degenerated, because the electors of Central Finsbury have elected a Native of India as their member in Parliament. I am not surprised that the *Pioneer* thinks so because degenerate minds always see degeneracy before them. (Laughter and cheers.) But the electors of Central Finsbury may well and truly reply that their action, so far from showing that they have degenerated, proves that they have risen to the height of true statesmanship and are alive to those conditions, the observance of which alone can secure the permanence of British rule in India. They may safely appeal to the voice of history on the subject to show that a great Empire can never be preserved by small and selfish minds. A well-known historian of the Roman Empire has truly pointed out this to be the great lesson taught by the history of the Romans "that it is the condition of permanent dominion that the conquerors should absorb the conquered gradually into their own body by extending, as circumstances arise, a share in their own exclusive privileges to the masses from whom they have torn their original independence." And then the same historian goes on to say, " All conquering nations feel an instinctive repugnance to making this sacrifice of pride and immediate interests, all struggle blindly against the necessity. Those alone who in due season submit to it retain the permanence of their institution and counteract the inherent principle of decay." Judge the action of the electors of Central Finsbury by this infallible test laid down by history, and we may well say that action they have shown that they know well how to preserve the Empire, of which England is the proud mistress, and, therefore, their generous action is eminently fitted to shine on the historian's page. (Loud cheers.) We are proud of Mr. Dadabhai, and he has made us proud of the electors of Central Finsbury ; and the electors of Central Finsbury in their turn have made us more than ever proud of the British Government under which we live, and whose blessings we enjoy and appreciate. (Loud and prolonged cheers.) Till the 7th of July 1892, history will record, England and India stood together hand in hand. On that memorable day the two sisters embraced each other—(cheers—)became more united in words and in deed than ever they had been before, and when I picture to myself the fact of Mr. Dadabhai's election, I feel as if England was now saying to India : "Sister, let no power be able to separate us two, whom an All-Wise Providence has thus drawn closer together." (Loud cheers.) And India sincerely, joyously, and loyally reciprocates the noble feeling thus inspired. And it is with that feeling, uppermost in my mind at this moment, that I now ask you to carry this Resolution unanimously, not only with all the generous enthusiasm you are capable of, but with all honours, that is, by standing up. (Loud cheers.)

The audience responded to the appeal with great enthusiasm by standing up to amen, and joyously waving their umbrellas and handkerchiefs.

Mr. D. E. Wacha, who was loudly cheered, said:—

Gentlemen, considering the enthusiasm and the profound feeling of unanimity which seems to pervade this unprecedentedly large assemblage, representing all that is the best and most influential, and all that is the most cultured and enlightened, in the community of this great city, of which we are all so proud, I take it for granted, that the resolution I am now going to move will be adopted by an acclamation and a chorus of cheers equal in intensity and loudness to the two preceding ones. Nothing affords me greater pride and pleasure than to stand before you this evening and be the medium of submitting for your acceptance that resolution. It runs as follows :—"That a committee, composed of the following gentlemen, be appointed to draw and forward addresses to Mr. Dadabhai Naoroji and the electors of Central Finsbury embodying the above resolutions, and to collect subscriptions to defray Mr. Dadabhai's election expenses :—Sir D. M. Petit,

chairman, Sir Jamesetjee Jejeebhoy, Messrs. Budroodin
Tyabjee, Framjee Dinshaw Petit, J. N. Tata, S. S.
Bengalee, Javerilal U. Yajnik, P. M. Mehta, N. J.
Chandravarkar, A. M. Dharamsi, D. Gostling, B. M. Malabari,
B. D. Petit, D. E. Wacha, Vandravandas Purshotumdas,
Vijbookundas Atmaram, Sorabjee Framjee Patel, R. M.
Sayani, Amirudin Tyabji, Fazulbhoy Visram, Curimbhoy
Ebrahim and Fazulbhoy Jeemabhoy Laljee; Drs. K. N.
Bahadurji and Cunha; Messrs. W. A. Chambers, Ruttonjee Bomanjee, H. M. Chichgur, Darasha R. Chichgur,
Damodurdas Thakursey Moolji, Tribhowandas Vurjivundas, Daji Abaji Khare, Jamietram N. Haridas,
Chimanlal H. Sitalwad, Wasoodev J. Kirtikar, Maneksha
J. Taleyarkhan, Ebrahim Rahimtola, Budrudin A. Kur,
Gordhundas Khatac Makanji, J. E. Modi, Jehanghir K.
R. Kama, Gordhundas G. Tejpal, Messrs. Ganesham
Nilkanth, Eknath R. Khote, Jugmohundas Vandravandas,
Alna Munji and Hasumbhai Visram; Drs. T. Blaney, A.
G. Viegas and Bhalchandra Krishna, and many others.

I am sure, gentlemen, it will meet with your unanimous
commendation. Eloquently does it speak for itself. And
with equal eloquence does it appeal to your liberality. It
is in the fitness of things and in the order of sequence that
our congratulations to the *First Indian* member of the
British House of Commons, and our grateful thanks to those
high-minded gentlemen of Central Finsbury, whose suffrages have secured his entry there, should be conveyed in
language suitable to the occasion. I dare say the combined
literary efforts of the· Committee will be equal to the task
of faithfully echoing the sentiments and joyous feelings
expressed at this meeting, and I dare say you all assembled
here will also endeavour to discharge your duty by generously responding to the pecuniary appeal. (Hear, hear,
and applause.) It is the least which we ought all to do,
considering the immense sacrifices undergone by Mr.
Dadabhai during the last five years, midst vicissitudes of
a most formidable character, which might have appalled a
man of less resolute determination and abiding faith,
in order to achieve that honourable ambition for the welfare
of his country. In fact, I cannot help remarking that we
would be woefully wanting in our duty if we failed at this
juncture to lighten, in however small a measure, the load
of the heavy sacrifices he has undergone in order to be
duly elected. If Bombay a few years ago nobly discharged

her duty in this direction towards the late lamented and
ever to be remembered Professor Fawcett, can she do less
for Mr. Dadabhai, her own son, the flesh of her flesh, and
the bone of her bone! (Cheers.) Not that he will be any
way the richer for such aid. But it is only meet that we
should in some measure testify to the spirit in which he has
nobly and unselfishly undergone a variety of sacrifices, and
I believe you will agree with me that we cannot express in
a more tangible form our own appreciation of that dis-
interestedness than in the way it is proposed in the resolution. Speaking of Mr. Fawcett, I am reminded, gentlemen, of that great meeting which was held in this very
hall seven years ago to commemorate his departed worth.
There is a curious but remarkable interest attached to it,
which I cannot but refer to here. That meeting was
presided by Lord Reay,—(Cheers)—the Governor of
Bombay, a Governor whose like, I fear, we may not see for
many a year to come. This is not the time and place to
speak of his sterling qualities as one of those rare and able
administrators who have ruled over this important Presidency since the days of Mountstuart Elphinstone. (Cheers.)
Mr. Dadabhai Naoroji was one of the principal speakers.
Who could have then foreseen that in a few short years
the citizen would seek the suffrages of a British constituency to enter Parliament; and that the Governor of the
day would be the person most actively sympathising with
him and according all his support and influence to enable
him to gain the honourable distinction? And yet these
events have happened and are a matter of history. The
incident to my mind has a deep significance for Indian
administrators and Indian people alike. But even more
unique than this incident is the other, which occurs to my
mind. India, from the Himalaya to Cape Comorin, and
from Calcutta to Karrachee, mourned over the fate by
which she was deprived of the unbought and invaluable
services of Professor Fawcett. (Cheers.) Such were his
sterling services, such his independent, yet judicious,
advocacy of the interests of the voiceless millions, whom
he had never seen in his life, that he was the first English
politician who earned the deserved sobriquet of the member
for India. Who could have then thought that time
in its ceaseless course would replace the English member
for India by a genuine son of the soil, a true-born,
patriotic representative Indian, the admired of all

admirers, the beloved of all, the one Indian whom the
country by universal acclaim thundered forth, as it were,
as the fittest person to take his seat in the British House
of Commons. (Loud cheers.) Is there not sufficient reason
to rejoice in this great historical event? Is India not
gratified that at last an indigenous son, by his intrepid
energy, indomitable perseverance, John Bull tenacity of
purpose, and thoroughly unselfish character having knocked
hard at the gates of St. Stephen's, is cheerfully bade to
enter them. But though the gratification is natural under
the circumstances, the one important fact in connection
with the election should never be lost sight of. Mr. Dadá-
bhai is a Liberal member of the Finsbury constituency
first. It is in that capacity alone he enters Parliament.
It is not as if India has returned him; though India will
be nearest to his heart. He will have a double and most
onerous duty to discharge, first, to his constituency, then
to India. This aspect is an anomaly by itself. It is one
of those singular anomalies to which the far-sighted and
thoughtful Mr. Yule had ably drawn attention in that
ever-memorable Allahabad address. The Englishman, who
is an elector in England, and who, therefore, enjoys all
the privileges which the British constitution confers on
him, is disqualified the moment he sets his foot on Indian
soil. He feels the deprivation of free citizenship. He
cannot return members to our Legislative Councils, a
solemn farce as they are, nay, not even under the modified
Councils Bill would he have that privilege. (Hear, hear.)
This anomaly in reference to English electors in India is
heightened by the entry of Mr. Dadabhai Naoroji into Parliament. The singular spectacle is presented of an
Indian gentleman, who is disqualified in India from taking
any part in its legislature unless he is considered "safe"
by our tremulous mediocrities and temporarily invited to
sit at the legislative board, could, if he has the pluck, the
energy, and the ability, gain admittance into the first
deliberative assembly of the world, take part in its proceedings and votes. Therein lies the anomaly which we all
hope will be removed. (Cheers.) In fact, were the
example which has now been set by Mr. Dadabhai to be
judiciously followed by half-a-dozen able and capable
Indians, our rulers would at once see the anomaly of the
present constitution, and hasten to repair it in another
way, the advantage would be this. Half-a-dozen Indians

6

fairly discussing current politics in the House of Commons would convince even the most chaotic Tory that the black men of Lord Salisbury are in no way inferior to the white men who legislate at St. Stephen's. And thus the foundations of rudimentary representative institutions in India would be widened. If the three hundred millions of India, from every corner of the Empire, from the gates, so to say, of the East to the gates of the West, from far off Mandalay to distant Quetta, are giving expressions to the same feelings and sentiments which we are expressing in this hall with a unanimity and spontaneity, which, I believe, are unparalleled in the history of the British Indian Empire, is not that a cause for reasonable pride and exultation ? The gladsome rejoicings which are taking place in every city, town and village are the outcome of the genuine recognition of the worth of this historical Indian. Save when the beloved Marquis of Ripon departed these shores,—(cheers)—India has never witnessed such manifestations of the unprompted impulses of her people, as in the present case. The Victorian era, gentlemen, has been memorable in the annals of the world for many events of the highest importance to the welfare of humanity. But I make bold to say that the joyous event, full of great political significance to this country in the future, will render that brilliant era even more memorable, nay, it will be imperishable. (Cheers.) It is the new India of Queen Victoria which is answerable for it, and India could not at this day show a worthier Indian than Mr. Dadabhai Naoroji as the product of the free and enlightened policy laid down by her statesmen for the better welfare of her people fifty years ago. Renewed cheers., I take, gentlemen, the British Indian Government to be a kind of beneficent terrestrial Providence. No doubt, like all things of the earth, it is full of imperfections. Its faults of omission and commission are as thick as dust. But in spite of it, it is a beneficent despotism, of which the world has seen no parallel. It stands to India in the position of *loco parentis*. Its object is to govern for the sake of the governed. Therefore, the success of its policy must be judged by the extent to which the subject population are educated in the act of self-government. The ideal of the parent must permeate the whole of England's relations alike with " her kin beyond the sea" and the subject populations of her greatest dependency. In this ideal

alone, which is being slowly carried out in practice, lies
the political regeneration of India—a regeneration which
shall redound to the glory of Englishmen in the world's
history for ever. Gentlemen, it is superfluous to refer
to the public career of Mr. Dadabhai, now extending over
well-nigh forty years. But it may be remarked with
justice that if any Indian, more than another, has fami-
liarised the British public during the same period with
the various aspects of Indian administration, and suggested
improvements for a better government, advantageous
alike to the governed and the governors, it is Mr. Dadabhai. It is to him India owes all the progress she has
made in the matter of the employment of our countrymen
in the higher offices of the State. It is to him she is indebted for the long agitation which resulted in the statute
of 1870, now rudely cast aside; and to the still later
agitation which led to the appointment of the Public Service Commission. It is also he who has kept alive the
burning controversy regarding the growing impoverish-
ment of the country and the series of great economic evils
resultingt herefrom. We shall have to keep in view these
matters. For if Indian economics and Indian finance are
again to be handled on the floor of the House of Commons
with the accuracy and judicial impartiality of the late Mr.
Fawcett, we may rely on Mr. Dadabhai. Closely connected
as I have been with him in these studies for many a year,
I can say without fear of being challenged that no Indian
is such a vast and accurate repository of facts on these
two subjects as he. Under the circumstances we have
reasons to hope, that if the new Parliament is to have at
all a fair lease of life, Mr. Dadabhai will be able to make
his mark there. Not that because one Indian has been
able to enter the House, therefore the millennium will
arrive. None is so sanguine as to expect it. But I am
strongly of conviction that with his characteristic devotion
to duty, his grasp of facts, his unerring accuracy, and,
above all, his convincing logic, he would be in a measure
instrumental in arresting the attention of the House to
questions of Indian finance, specially exchange and the
equitable distribution of those heavy military and other
burdens, with which this country is unjustly saddled and
other Indian problems in a larger degree than has been
the case hitherto. (Cheers.) Again, his tact and judgment
will stand him in good stead. This, I believe, he posses-

ses as much as the late lamented Mr. Bradlaugh. In fact,
gentlemen, it is to be hoped that it may be the good fortune
of Mr. Dadabhai to take up the thread of Indian politics
where that other distinguished English member for India
prematurely left it. There is hope that he will be able to
do so, bearing in mind that he shall have for his helpers
many of the old members in sympathy with India who
have been re-elected. We all greatly rejoice at the return
of Messrs. Caine, Schwann, Samuel Smith, Bryce, Reed,
and many others who have rendered admirable service to
us in the last Parliament. We cannot, however, but
deeply regret the defeat of two such sturdy champions of
Indian interests as Sir W. Wedderburn— cheers,—and
Mr. W. Digby. They were chiefly instrumental in helping
Mr. Dadabhai at Finsbury, and it is a bitter disappointment to us all that they have failed in their gallant fight.
With these two the trio would have been complete. At
any rate, we hope Mr. Dadabhai may be so far successful
as to carry out some of the minor financial reform which
the late Mr. Bradlaugh— cheers —left unaccomplished.
I especially refer to the discussion of the Indian budget
on a day early in June, instead of at the fag end of the
Session. This reform could only become practical when
the financial year is made coeval with the calendar year.
It would be impossible then for Finance Ministers to
complain of the " uncertainties of March," while it would
be in every way practical to present a financial statement
exhibiting complete accounts instead of only revised esti-
mates, which soon after turn surpluses into deficits, and
vice versâ. But, gentlemen, I have taken more of your
time than I expected, so that I will not detain you longer.
I will conclude my harangue with only one observation.
We have named Mr. Dadabhai as India's Grand Old Man.
Now, it is needful to say that in many public aspects of
the career of Mr. Gladstone, Mr. Dadabhai has closely re-
sembled. Some years ago Lord Selbourne, speaking of
Mr. Gladstone, observed regarding the marvellous popularity and the marvellous esteem in which he was held
by all classes of the British people,—I cannot do better
than quote his words, with but a slight change, regarding
the marvellous popularity of Mr. Dadabhai :—" It does not
lie in his great accomplishments, in his great ability,
though these commend themselves to our admiration."
(Loud cheers.) But the people of India understand him.

They know " that he has profound sympathy with them ;
that. he has nothing at heart but truly to promote their
interests, according to his honest views of them ; and
whether we judge rightly or wrongly about this question
or that, and, of course, all of us are liable to error, none
pretend to infallibility ; they know that he is a man who
is actuated only by the purest motives, and that he presents
the highest example of public and of private integrity."
(Cheers.)

This, gentlemen, you will admit, is a faithful picture of
Mr. Dadabhai. Such being the case, let us all wish in the
inspiriting lines of Mr. Punch's poets, slightly altered, that
he may be long spared to India for India's true welfare ;
for he is really " One in a million," as an Anglo-Indian
journalist observed years ago :—

> " Our's is no stripling ; no Knight of the Carpet
> Him, of the People, pet.
> Years cannot fetter nor foes make afraid
> Firm as the fixed rock,
> Braving the tempest's shock.
> Faster he roots him the fiercer it blows.
> England and India then
> Echo his praise again."

(Loud and prolonged cheers.)

Mr. A. M. Dharamsi said :—

Mr. Chairman and Gentlemen,—I have much pleasure
in seconding the resolution proposed by my friend, Mr.
Wacha, and I have no doubt that it will meet with your
hearty approval. Gentlemen, it is needless for me to say
that it is our bounden duty on this occasion to forward an
address of congratulation to Mr. Dadabhai, expressing our
feelings of joy and gratification at his election to a seat in
the British Parliament. The occasion is, indeed, rare and
unique. (Hear, hear.) The news of Mr. Dadabhai's
success sent a thrill of joy throughout the country, and all
classes of the community have with singular unanimity
combined to show their deep respect for Mr. Dadabhai,
and their sense of appreciation of his lifelong services in
the cause of his country and its people. (Cheers.) That
this should be so is natural. Gentlemen, all of us are
acquainted more or less with Mr. Dadabhai's work. From
his early days he imposed upon himself the task of being
useful to his country and of promoting its social, intellectual,

and political advancement. (Applause.) He has been most instrumental in bringing the wants and aspirations of India before the English people, and of exciting attention in England about Indian matters by writing to English journals and magazines, by addressing public bodies and associations, and by carrying on correspondence on important subjects, concerning India with the authorities in England. He has rendered invaluable service to the country at large, and has laid its people under a deep debt of gratitude. (Cheers.) His single-mindedness, unselfishness, zeal, energy, perseverance, and earnestness of purpose are beyond all praise. He is a model of a true patriot, and his life and career cannot but command our respect and admiration—nay, inspire us with a feeling of deference. (Gentlemen, it is not necessary to dwell at large upon the great advantages which must arise to India by the British Parliament having correct information about the real condition and wants of this country. And who can be better qualified than Mr. Dadabhai to speak with authority on these matters, to enlighten the British public in regard thereto and to correct erroneous impressions? As financier, as an economist, as an educationalist, as a statesman and a politician, Mr. Dadabhai has shown that he is possessed of singular qualifications and abilities which will undoubtedly stand him in good stead in the high and honourable position in which Providence has now placed him. (Cheers.) When the efforts of Mr. Dadabhai to get into Parliament have been crowned with success, I say it is incumbent upon us to vote him a congratulatory address expressing the sentiments of regard and esteem that we entertain for him and of the feelings of unbounded joy that his success has caused in our hearts. Gentlemen, Mr. Dadabhai has worked disinterestedly, and at considerable self-sacrifice, and it is only reasonable that his election expenses should be defrayed by us. This is the least that we owe him. (Cheers) Before I conclude, gentlemen, I wish to say a word about the obligations under which the electors of Central Finsbury have laid this country by electing Mr. Dadabhai as their representative in Parliament. Gentlemen, the high-mindedness of these electors cannot be spoken of too highly. It furnishes a noble example of the broad tolerance worthy of England and her sons. (Cheers.) To them our best and heartfelt thanks are due, and it is our duty to send them an address also. The Committee you are asked to appoint is a strong and influential one, and I have no doubt they will do their work in a satisfactory manner. (Loud cheers.)

The resolution was then carried with acclamation.

Mr. H. A. Wadia, barrister of Kattywar, said :—

Mr. Chairman and Gentlemen,—I have been asked to propose, and I feel it on this occasion a privilege to propose, the following resolution :—" That the thanks of this meeting be conveyed to the Most Noble the Marquis of Ripon and to the other ladies and gentlemen who accorded their sympathy and support to Mr. Dadabhai Naoroji in his election. I am sure, gentlemen, there is no one who will acknowledge more than Mr. Dadabhai Naoroji himself how indispensable to his sustained and successful struggle were the sympathy and support of the friends who in helping Mr. Dadabhai have helped us all and laid us all under an enduring obligation. We have only to remember the seven long years of alternating hopes and fears, of great confidence at one time and of still greater despair more often, and then reflect if the man whose success gives us so much to hope for and so much to rejoice at could possibly have gone through—was he with all his fortitude and his serenity—all that he had to and did go through—without the unswerving support and the hearty and unflinching sympathy which only Englishmen and women know how to give to a cause they espouse. I cannot pretend on this occasion to name all our kind friends, or to enumerate all their kind efforts. But there are some names which must be mentioned, and foremost among them in our hearts and on our lips must be the name of him whose name and fame will be imperishable in India— for if ever there was a man risen to supreme power who believed and acted in this belief that he held his great commission,

> From that supernal Judge who stirs good thoughts
> In any breast of strong authority,

impartial history will record that the man and ruler was the Most Noble the Marquis of Ripon. (Cheers.) We knew, and we expected, that where India's true rights and interests were concerned, Lord Ripon's help was secured, and, gentlemen, I am only mentioning the fact when I say that Lord Ripon's sympathy and support was un-

surpassed by those of any other friend. **This adds one
more** to his many obligations, and brings back to us more
keenly and gratefully than ever the recollections of his
righteous rule. Next to Lord Ripon's name I will mention
the name of Lord Reay, if only for this reason—that the
Ripon-Reay combination has a peculiar fascination. It
fascinates even Mr. Maclean. But, Sir, we in Bombay must
feel a peculiar joy in knowing that our friend was so generously and heartily befriended by our late Governor. I must
also mention the names of the Earl of Aberdeen and the Earl
of Rosebery. Lord Aberdeen's cordial sympathy with subject nations is well known. As for Lord Rosebery, all I
will say on this occasion is, that by his constant sympathy
and his earnest desire to see Mr. Dadadhai successful in
entering Parliament, the noble Earl has taught India to feel
some share—humble no doubt but sincere—in the rising
hopes and great expectations which the Empire at large
feels and entertains in regard to him. (Cheers.) There
are many other names I would like to mention, but time
will not permit my doing so, but mentioning that of
Professor Bryce, of Mr. William Digby, and last, but
not least, of Sir William Wedderburn. (Loud cheers.)
I am sure, Sir, all India is as much disappointed at Sir
William's failure as it has rejoiced in Mr. Dadabhai's
success. We can only wish and pray that he soon may
have another chance, and succeed at last in entering
Parliament where he will help our cause as only he can.
The resolution speaks of the help of English ladies also.
There are some ladies of whom I am sorry I have not the
permission to speak openly. They have been silent work-
ers in our cause, and I am sure, gentlemen, the honour to
them and our obligation to them are all the greater. But
there is one name which we must remember not only with
gratitude, but with peculiar pride. It is of that great and
good English lady who for forty years, since at Scutari
she passed through the gathering gloom and flitted from
room to room on her true woman's mission, has stood
before the world as the poet sang she would stand in
England's annals,—

> A noble type of good
> Heroic womanhood.

—I mean Miss Florence Nightingale. (Prolonged cheers.)
I am sure Mr. Dadabhai must have felt it a privilege to

have her sympathy and support, and, Sir, I know not in
what words to describe what we must feel when we think
that neither age nor infirmities prevent her from sending
to us across the seas messages of sympathy and solicitude
peculiarly her own, and befriending our cause in a manner
which no other living woman can. There is another lady
whose name I must mention—and that is the name of
Mrs. Evans Bell. I have been told that no man or woman
worked with greater fervour, zeal, or energy and industry
than this lady. From shop to shop, from house to house
she went using her influence courting votes and befriending
our cause in various ways; and to her efforts in a great
measure is due the victory which Mr. Dadabhai won. Her
friendship for our friend brings back to our memory the
name and work of her deceased husband, than whom
India, when he lived, had no better or more devoted friend.
And it will give her satisfaction, I am sure, to know that
what she did has revived his memory so gratefully among
us. I have told you the names of some of these friends.
I must now ask you to bear in mind what these friends
have done for us, so that we may be adequately mindful
of what is due from us in return. They had through many
difficulties and against much obloquy pledged their credit
with their countrymen on our behalf. They have, in the
first place, assured their countrymen of our devoted loyalty.
As for our loyalty, standing in this hall and surrounded
by such citizens, I feel, Sir, that it is not necessary to
speak much. But this I will say to those who trust us, and
to those who do not, that ours is a sincere and abiding
loyalty, for it springs from our innate conviction that
loyalty to our country's cause is consistent only with
loyalty to our country's sovereign, and that those who
would for one moment entertain any thought of disloyalty
to Britain's rule in India are traitors to India's best interests and faithless to India's fairest hopes. Gentlemen,
our friends have done more. They have pledged their
credit that after enjoying so long the benefits of a just
government, we have been trained to become worthy of,
and we have become entitled to claim the benefits of a
reasonable amount of freedom, and that such freedom
might be extended to us, not only with absolute security
to Britain's rule, but also with greater credit to Great
Britain and greater happiness and prosperity to India. It
is not our thanks these friends will appreciate so much as

7

our efforts to help them in redeeming such pledges. Are we ready to do so? It depends on our champion then in England, and on our efforts—our united efforts—here in India. As for him we have no doubt. Whether you ask for ability and integrity, or knowledge or experience, whether you call for the great virtues that distinguish a public career, or the less difficult virtues that adorn and ennoble private life, no individual Indian could respond to that call so fittingly and so completely as Dadabhai Naoroji. His success comes providentially and fittingly to crown a career of singular probity, of extraordinary self-denial, of unceasing usefulness, and of unexampled devotion to his country's cause. We know that his services are secured to our country as long as life lasts. Let us, therefore, be thankful and pray to God to give him strength and health and long life for his great task. He will not only represent our interests and hopes, but all that is good and great and beneficent and glorious in British rule. When he sits there India will look to him with hopes, and trust that England too may point to him with pride and triumph, for he will sit there to press to the world that Britain's rule does not enslave but upraises and exalts. The real question is, will we be true to our duty? That is the question our friends will ask you to reply to, not by words but by deeds, not in eloquent demonstration but well sustained and permanent efforts. Gentlemen, let us not only thank them, but assure them that we know what they have done for us, understand what they want from us, and are prepared to do our duty to them and to India. That duty India has the right to demand from us never more urgently than now, when the first line has been written in a new and more eventful chapter of her history, and, Sir, I will add that duty India claims or expects from us never more hopefully than now when her sons all over this vast land, unmoved by the differences which distinguish but do not divide us, men of different creeds—inheritors of varied traditions—descendants of distinct races—yet sprung from the same soil—subjects of the same sovereign, and soldiers in the same cause—are acclaiming with united voice and heart—the success of one deserving and trusted brother, seeing in it what they believe is and what they pray, may prove to be for their country the harbinger of a brighter and a better day. (Loud and prolonged cheers.) .

Mr. Narayan Vishnu Gokhale said :—

Mr. President and gentlemen,—I feel great pleasure in seconding the resolution which stands in my name. During the last three weeks there have been rejoicings and demonstrations throughout the country inconnection with Mr. Dadabhai's success in Central Finsbury. We, too, have met this evening to give articulate expression to our feeling of joy and satisfaction. But in this hour of national congratulation we cannot allow ourselves to forget the claims to our cordial gratitude of the several high-souled Englishmen and generous-hearted English women who supported his candidature during the arduous struggle he so courageously maintained—(cheers)—for nearly six years. In a speech delivered by Mr. Dadabhai at the Ripon Club, he asked his audience to act upon a golden precept which is so strikingly exemplified in his remarkable public career. The precept was " Persevere should be our motto, no matter how often we may be disappointed." (Hear, hear.) The observation reminds me of an interesting story which appropriately illustrates the history of Mr. Dadabhai's candidature. Diogenes offered himself as a disciple to Antisthenes. He was refused, but still persisted. The cynic threatened to strike him if he did not depart. " Strike," said Diogenes, " you will not find a stick hard enough to conquer my perseverance." Antisthenes was overcome, and forthwith accepted him as his pupil. Though Mr. Dadabhai's invincible resolution and profound earnestness thus enabled him to vanquish all opposition, and led him to victory, one can easily imagine how at times even his sanguine soul must have experienced a pang of keen disappointment owing to cold indifference or unexpected opposition on the part of those who had promised to support him. It was on occasions like these that the kindly sympathy and encouragement of his English friends sustained him in his resolution to pursue the goal of his lofty and patriotic ambition. (Cheers.) To them our cordial thanks are due. Among the several noble-minded ladies who took warm interest in Mr. Dadabhai are to be found the names of Mrs. Josephine Butler, Miss Colenso, and Miss Florence Nightingale—that distinguished philanthropist who has done so much by her disinterested exertions to arouse the interest of the people of India and England in the question of sanitary reform. To all of them we owe a deep debt of gratitude. Among the distinguished

Englishmen who accorded their sympathy and support to our esteemed countryman there is the revered name of that Viceroy whose memory is enshrined in the hearts of the people of this country, and who has immortalized himself in the pages of modern Indian history by his policy of justice, equality, and righteousness. On the eve of his departure from India Lord Ripon told the people of Lahore that he had governed the country, not as a ruler, but as friend, and it is a source of genuine satisfaction to us all that he has continued taking the same kindly interest in our welfare. (Cheers.) Then there is among the sympathisers of Mr. Dadabhai the illustrious name of Lord Reay, who was to this Presidency what Ripon, the righteous, was to the entire country,—(cheers)—and also the name of Mr. Gladstone, the greatest statesman of the century, who has in no small measure liberalized the political institutions of England and has done not a little to help fallen nationalities. (Loud cheers.) The services of these great Englishmen and those of many others whose names it would take long to recapitulate, deserve to be gratefully acknowledged. Gentlemen, the memorable event which we are assembled here to-night to commemorate has a profound significance of its own, and opens a vista of untold possibilities which it would be out of place for me to dwell upon at this moment. Before the arrival of Lord Ripon to this country Western thought and education had already communicated the Promethean spark to the dormant forms of our national life. It was his viceroyalty that kindled the spark into a blazing flame. (Cheers.) It was under his *régime* that the dry bones in the open valley became instinct with life. It was his liberal administration that imparted a powerful impetus to the unifying forces already at work in the country. These beneficent influences, thus strengthened and intensified, have gathered increasing strength year after year, have manifested themselves in various forms of social and political activity, and are destined to play no small part in the moral and intellectual elevation of India. They have awakened the political conscience of the people and kindled in their breasts a keen sense of national unity. With the return of Mr. Dadabhai to Parliament with the help and encouragement of our well-wishers in England, we have, during the last fortnight, realized more fully and vividly than we had ever done before how all of us form an inseparable part of the stately fabric of her Majesty's empire, how we are the subjects of the same sovereign, the co-parceners of the same rights and privileges, linked together by a common destiny and having a common rôle to enact in history. All thoughtful Englishmen will acknowledge that this is no small step towards the consolidation and unification of England's world-wide empire. Gentlemen, I will tell you presently how the assistance of India's well-wishers is likely to be of very great use to us in another direction. The machinery of Indian government has become so unwieldy, and in consequence so slow to move, and the actual work of administration is becoming so increasingly difficult that even a talented, sympathetic, and conscientious administrator scarcely ventures to rise to the level of constructive statesmanship. As years roll on the conviction is gradually growing upon me that the stimulus must come from without even for the purpose of effecting small reforms. Besides there are certain fundamental questions involving administrative changes of a more or less organic character which can only be fought out on the floor of the English House of Commons with the support of our staunch friends in England. But before these triumphs can be achieved, we must awaken the people of England to a sense of their responsibility towards this vast dependency. Mr. Dadabhai's successful candidature has excited unusual interest even in England, and there can be no doubt that a growing band of philanthropic Englishmen will, in course of time, be found willing to work the small lever we have succeeded in fixing there within the last few years. Only let us be prepared to wield with effect our lever here by forgetting like Mr. Dadabhai our sectional and racial differences, and by co-operating with one heart and soul with our friends in England. Let the words "loyalty, unity, perseverance and self-sacrifice" be inscribed on our banner, and then we need not despair of our future. (Cheers.) For the kindly and sympathetic interest taken by our English friends in Indian affairs we are one and all thankful to them, and I will now ask you, gentlemen, to join our countrymen in the other parts of the empire in sending our message of heart felt gratitude to those noble-hearted ladies and gentlemen through whose support and encouragement our much esteemed citizen has been enabled to enter the House of Commons, and to fulfil the noble ideal of the poet who sung

" If thou can'st plan a noble deed,
And never flag till it succeed,
Though in the strife thy heart should bleed,
Whatever obstacles control,
Thine honr will come—go on true soul,
Thou'lt win the prize, thou'lt reach the goal."

(Loud cheers.) With the permission of the chairman, a Punjabee gentleman here recited verses composed in the Hindustani language in honour of Mr. Dadabhai Naoroji and the electors of Central Finsbury, which he delivered with pathos and actions suiting to the words. The Punjabee gentleman was loudly cheered by the meeting.

On the motion of Mr. Damodhur Thakersey Muljee, seconded by the Cazee Sheriff Mohomed Saheb, of Bombay, a hearty vote of thanks was passed to the chairman.

At the suggestion of Mr. P. M. Mehta, three cheers were given for her Majesty the Queen-Empress, which were responded to most vociferously, after which the proceedings terminated at about 7 P.M.

2. Public Meeting in Madras.

A public meeting of the Native Community of Madras was held last evening at Patcheappa's Hall, for the purpose of giving expression to the gratitude they felt to the electors of Central Finsbury, for returning Mr. Dadabhai Naorojoi to Parliament, and of conveying their congratulations to Mr. Dadabhai Naoroji. The hall was packed to its utmost limit, many shop-keepers of the adjoining China bazaar, Kotwal chavadi, and Goojilly attending the meeting having closed their shops. The outside of the hall was tastefully illuminated with rows of coloured lights and there was a general look of rejoicing about the hall. The assembly represented every section of the community, and all evinced the greatest enthusiasm in the proceedings, listening attentively to the speeches and cheering the speakers to the echo. Amongst those present were Messrs. P. Somasundaram Chetty, Hon. Mir Humayunjah Bahadur, c.i.e., Sir T. Muthusami Iyer, Kt., c.r.e., Rajah T. Rama Rao, R. Balaji Rao, Rai Bahadur P. Anunda Charlu, N. Subramaniam, Rajah Sir Savalai Ramaswami Mudelly, Kt., c.i.e., Dewan Bahadur R. Ragoonath Rao, Dewan Bahadur Subramania Aiyar, c.i.e., Hon'ble V. Bashyam Aiyangar, C. Yethirajulu Naidu, M. O. Parthasarady

Iyengar, P. Theagaroya Chetty, G. Subramania Iyer, G.
Mahadeva Chetty, Krishna Doss Balamukun Doss, W. S.
Venkataramanjulu Naidu, M. Varadarajulu Chetty, P. V.
Krishnasami Chetty, M. Abboy Naidu, S. Pulney Andy, M.
Venugopala Pillai, C. S. Thiyagaraya Mudelly, T. V.
Apparao Naidu, K. P. Visvanatha Aiyar, M. Ethiraja
Pillai, K. P. Sankara Menon, S. Appasami Chetty, R. N.
Prakasa Mudelliar, M. Ramakrishna Pantulu, V. R.
Basoova Pillai, M. Cuppusami Chetti, P. Ethirajulu Naidu,
M. Govindu Chetty, P. M. Sivagnana Mudelly, Ahmed
Hussien, T. R. Ramanada Aiyar, V. Krishnasami Aiyar,
P. S. Sivaswami Aiyar, M. Venkataramiah Chetty, V.
Runga Chari, M. Thirumala Chari, P. R. Sundaram Aiyar,
C. Ethirajulu Chetty, A. C. Parthasarady Naidu, P.
Subramania Aiyar, M. Krishnama Chari, Balakristna Doss,
K. Ethiraja Pillay, C. R. Tiruvenkata Chari, R. Bala-
kristnama Chetti, M. Ramasami Naidu, P. Subramania
Chetti, Subramyya Chetti, V. C. Sesha Chari, C. Subbiah
Chetti, K. Subba Row, M. Veeraraghava Chari, M. E.
Sreerunga Chariar, B. Panchapicura Sastriar, V. Deshika
Chari, V. Seshadari, C. Runga Row, S. Gurusamy Chetty,
M. A. Parthasarty Iyengar, M. Tirumala Chariar, P. T.
Narasimha Chariar, T. V. Seshagheri Iyer, and Rai
Bahadur C. V. Cunniah Chetty, &c. &c.

On the motion of Rajah Sir Savalay Ramsawmy
Mudaliar, seconded by Mr. Venugopal Pillai, Mr. P. Soma-
soondram Chetty was voted to the Chair.

The Chairman opened the meeting in the following words:—

Fellow-Citizens of the Town of Madras, Gentlemen,—
An event of a most joyful and auspicious character has
called us together here this evening, and it is to me, personally, a source of peculiar pride and satisfaction that I
have to take part in the proceedings of this interesting
meeting. The event that we are assembled to rejoice
over and celebrate is unique in character, and not unlikely
to be far reaching in its consequences. No argument is
needed to show its uniqueness. For the latter end of this
nineteenth century has been reserved the great and
imperishable glory of showing that country, which was
the first in the world to emancipate the slave, to remove
religious disabilities, to discourage protective duties, and
to govern subject nations with humanity and justice, is

also the first to establish and to illustrate the political
equality of the ruling Briton and the ruled Native of
India, by assigning to a distinguished son of India a seat
in the British House of Commons, the great palladium of
British liberty and British justice. Your first duty this
evening is to express your profound and heartfelt gratitude to the electors of Central Finsbury for the magnanimous impartiality displayed by them in appreciating at
their true worth the virtues and merits of Mr. Dadabhai
Naoroji, and in conferring on India the priceless boon of
a most persevering and unflinching advocate of Indian
interests, while securing for themselves a representative
of extensive knowledge and experience in matters commercial, industrial and political, and of unswerving
integrity and firmness of purpose. Your next duty is to
offer your most cordial congratulations to Mr. Dadabhai
Naoroji on the proud distinction that he has earned, and
to thank him from the bottom of your hearts for all the
good he has already done to India. I may go on endlessly,
gentlemen, if it is right for me to anticipate what I have
no doubt the speakers entrusted with the second and third
resolutions will dilate upon with far greater force and
vigorous eloquence than I can. I shall, therefore, content
myself with calling upon the Hon'ble Mir Humayun Jah
Bahadur to move the second resolution.

It was proposed by the Hon'ble Mir Humayun Jah
Bahadur :—"That this meeting feels deeply thankful to
the electors of Central Finsbury for electing Mr. Dadabhai
Naoroji as their representative in Parliament, and for
setting a noble example of large-hearted sympathy and
generous appreciation of merit without reference to race,
creed or colour."

The proposer said :—

Gentlemen,—During a period of over 33 years past, I
have been present at almost all public meetings in this city,
but do not remember seeing a more enthusiastic gathering
than the present one. This in itself is a proof that natives
of India, as a rule, are not ungrateful even for the smallest
consideration ever shown them, as all of you have come
here to-night with the sole object to offer your warm and
grateful thanks to the Liberal electors of Central Finsbury
for having chosen Mr. Dadabhai Naoroji, a highly distinguished and worthy son of India, to represent them in the

grandest assembly the world can boast of. The electors of our friend have thus given an excellent example how they can rise superior to local considerations, and prove to be disinterestedly magnanimous in the discharge of public duties to elect the best available candidate for Parliament, and stretch a friendly hand to India, for which all of us feel highly gratified and honoured. This memorable event of a Native of India being returned by an English constituency to represent them in the British Parliament is the first happy occurrence of its kind, and augurs well for the future. Having been brought about by a laudable spirit, it is expected to prove of great service to both countries, England and India, in equal measure in course of time. Words, however, cannot adequately convey our feelings, so without detaining you, I will conclude by remarking that in offering your thanks to the electors of Mr. Dadabhai, you are indirectly offering your thanks to that mystic power, unto whom the whole universe moves.

Mr. P. V. Krishnasawmy Chetty, in seconding the resolution, observed :—

Gentlemen,—I have the pleasure and the honour of seconding the resolution now moved by our esteemed fellow-citizen, Mir Humayun Jah Bahadur. It is a resolution, gentlemen, that appeals to an undoubted trait of our national character, for, gentlemen, 1 may say that we are nothing if we are not a grateful people. From various parts of the country have gone forth demonstrations of joy and gratitude—joy at the stroke of good fortune that came upon us as such an agreeable surprise, gratitude to those good men who contributed to the same. In those numerous tributes of thankfulness which have been addressed to the electors of Central Finsbury, gentlemen, whether couched in words of stirring eloquence as from Bombay, or in the mildest and briefest language, the same surcharged with feelings of an overflowing heart have found expression more or less adequate. While we have met here, gentlemen, to tender our acknowledgments to these high-minded electors, it is but fit that we pause for a moment and endeavour to realise what it is they have done and what is the character of their beneficent act that the native population of this vast Indian continent have so enthusiastically rejoiced over. It seems to me, gentlemen, that looking at it in its immensity what these 'good men and true' have done is

8

an act of political heroism, which, let us hope, will be
written in the future pages of history in characters of
gold. (Cheers.) Gentlemen, it has to be remembered that
in putting forward the candidature of our countryman,
Mr. Dadabhai Naoroji, in standing by and supporting it
through good and evil influences, and in bringing it to a
successful termination, these heroic electors went through
an ordeal of no small magnitude, an ordeal that might
have disheartened less courageous souls. They had as it
were, gentlemen, to raise themselves above themselves.
(Cheers.) They had to raise above tradition and prejudice,
tradition highly rigid in its exactions, prejudice so far
national, that it betrayed a cautious and highly esteemed
Prime Minister into a moment's weakness which must cost
him years of regret and repentance; they had to face
obloquy and misrepresentation; they had to withstand the
odium of critics, self-sufficient critics, whose denunciations
have gone the length of charging them with degeneracy.
Such, gentlemen, is the fate of some noble souls who look
ahead of their time in prophetic wisdom, and such fate
this devoted band of electors have manfully faced. In
electing their representative, the resolution now submitted
to you points out that they paid no heed to considerations
of race, creed, or colour. What race or races, what creed
or faith, what nationality did they limit their choice to?
Gentlemen, they assigned to themselves no such conven-
tional limits. One might well say, the only race they
would recognise in the largeness of their hearts was the
human race; the only creed they owned allegiance to was
their unshaken faith in the destiny of man to eternally
progress; the only colour their political eye would
perceive was the colour of capacity and character. And,
gentlemen, exercising their choice on so wide a field, they
only gave effect to a principle of enlightened statesmanship which has been proclaimed by statute and charter,
which has existed in theory during all these years, but
the reduction of which to practice has been naturally beset
with difficulties. Gentlemen, we owe it to the generosity
of British character and British statesmanship that rights
are accorded to us in theory, which might well raise the
envy of any non-British-governed nation. At the same
time, we owe it to the imperfections of human nature that
the recognition of those rights, in practice, is retarded or
obstructed in its due course. But, gentlemen, in the

fulness of time, the dictates of true and genuine statesmanship will, as they needs must, attain fruition, and in such
fulness of time, it has come to pass that the Liberal electors of Central Finsbury have returned to Parliament
as their representative the " black man," gentlemen, that
had been but recently signalised as such, authoritatively,
so to speak. And, gentlemen, this action of the electors
of Finsbury may be proclaimed from housetops as a standing remonstrance against the prejudice which is responsible
for such signalisation. It is when the conduct of these
electors is looked at in the light of these facts, it ennobles
them in the estimation of the unprejudiced world and
endears them to our countrymen. No doubt, gentlemen,
in electing Mr. Dadabhai Naoroji, the Liberal electors of
Central Finsbury have not been unmindful of their own
interests. The member they have returned is one of whom
any constituency may well be proud, upon whom any
constituency may, with confidence, rely for perfect probity,
unremitting devotion to duty, and a masterly capacity to
direct such devotion to the best of their interests. But,
it would not have been difficult for them to have found
from amongst their own countrymen willing aspirants for
the honour, possessed of Mr. Dadabhai Naoroji's qualifications. Yet, with a magnanimity truly sublime, they preferred our countryman to theirs. And, what is the result ?
We have now got, returned, to the House of Commons, to
that throne of grace, a countryman of ours, and that
countryman, Mr. Dadabhai Naoroji, whom the unanimous
voice of the country has for years marked out as *the man*
to represent her millions of population, *the man* to open
the repositories of his knowledge of her—the result of a
lifelong and devoted study—for the edification of that
House, and to give them the benefit of his matured coun-
sels. With Mr. Dadabhai Naoroji in the House of Commons, gentlemen, we are truly enabled to hope that it may
become impossible for the scandal to exist much longer or
any longer of empty benches being harangued to on the
Indian Budget. One more feature, gentlemen, of this
election, has to be noticed as doubling its value to us. It
comes to us most opportunely. It comes to us like a
Godsend at a time when we should otherwise be lost in disappointment at the failure of Sir W. Wedderburn and Mr.
Digby to be returned—a failure which we cannot too deeply
regret—a loss which we should otherwise be ill able to

bear. Our gratitude, therefore, gentlemen, is all the more enhanced by the relief these good electors have afforded us from the weight of that disappointment. I will not occupy more of your time, gentlemen, but confidently invite you to carry this resolution by acclamation.

The proposition was then put to the meeting and carried unanimously.

In proposing the next proposition, Rai Bahadur P. Ananda Charlu spoke as follows :—

Chairman and Fellow-Countrymen,—I have to place before you a threefold proposition. First, I ask you to affirm that the Native community of Madras feel deeply gratified to find that one of their fellow-countrymen is to have a seat in the British House of Commons. Secondly, I ask you to say that the Native community congratulate Mr. Dadabhai Naoroji on being the first to win that proud distinction (cheers); and, thirdly, I ask you to place on record that they feel grateful to Mr. Dadabhai Naoroji for his unselfish and untiring efforts on behalf of the people of India. (Cheers.) The first proposition, as you see, sets forth in emphatic terms the depth of pleasure with which we have received what, in the words of a leading English organ, is a message of fellow-citizenship from the millions in London to the millions in India. (Cheers.) It is, most unquestionably, the outcome of the direct rule of India by the Queen-Empress (cheers), and is a distinct acceptance, by a few thousand English electors, of the terms of equality between all the subjects of Her Majesty's wide Empire held forth in that magnificent State Paper which was issued when she took into her own hands the sovereignty of this country. (Cheers.) If this recognition came from the author of that promise, if it emanated from the Queen-Empress as a token of personal appreciation on her part, if it came in the way that the alphabetical and other birth-day honours come, the value and significance would not be one-tenth as great as now (cheers), for it may be said that the promiser would generally consider herself as bound to seek yearly redemption. But where, as in the present instance, the gracious word of hope was given by one, and it rested with others who are free to act as they please to give effect to it, the award has a peculiar worth of its own and cannot be discounted, even by the most carping critic, as the deed of one who is committed to it and who cannot,

out of a sense of honour, too long postpone it. (Cheers.)
The Native community are, therefore, justly entitled to rejoice that, in the recognition of merit, irrespective of considerations of race, colour, or creed, the words of a monarch
among monarchs, have received an emphatic and hearty
confirmation from the free electors of a British constituency
(cheers), and that thereby a Native of this country has
acquired the proud distinction of a seat in an assembly the
most powerful and the most august on the face of the
Globe. (Cheers.) To congratulate Mr. Dadabhai Naoroji
on winning that proud distinction is the purpose of the
second branch of my proposition. Though to Mr. Naoroji,
personally, it may be little more than a reward for patience
and perseverance—a reward which would have been his
prize in his prime of life as to many others, if he had
started in life in England without the inconvenient connection with a community looked down upon as a subject race,
it is nevertheless a signal success and a striking testimony,
as the *Bombay Gazette* has truly said, to his high character
and to the tact with which he combined stability of purpose
with an imperturbable serenity of mind and manner. The
mantle of a legislator for vast populations had worthily
fallen upon Mr. Dadabhai Naoroji several years ago when
he was chosen for a seat in the Legislative Council in
Bombay ; and I am not at all sure that his scope of usefulness
really is extended by reason of his taking his seat in the
British House of Commons. But it is in view to the *quality*
of service he will hereafter render rather than the *quantity*
of service from his new post of duty that I have an agreeable prospect. We congratulate Mr. Dadabhai Naoroji as
much for the proud distinction he has achieved as for the
bright prospect he holds forth of a kind of service, invaluable in worth and incalculable in results. With our distinguished countrymen, Mr. Mehta and with the *Bombay
Gazette*, let us wish Mr. Dadabhai Naoroji every success in
Parliament, and let us join them in their prediction that
whether it falls to his lot to do much or to do little in the
House of Commons, he will perform it with unselfish zeal
or devotion. (Cheers.) I am not sure if there are many
in this assembly who know Mr. Dadabhai Naoroji as inti-
mately as I have known him. If there are, I feel certain
that they will agree with me when I say that to see him, is
to like him, to mix with him, is to love him, to hear him,
for even a space of five minutes, is to admire and revere

him. (Cheers.) His is indeed not the oratory which knocks and enters. But exclusively his is the eloquence which is simplicity itself, and which, by the manner of telling, conciliates and disarms opposition, as if by means of a potent charm. He seems to be singularly conscious that—

Men must be taught as if you taught them not.
And things unknown proposed as things forgot.

It only remains now to call attention to the last branch of the proposition, and it records our gratitude to Mr. Dadabhai Naoroji in these words :—"The Native community feel grateful to him for his unselfish and untiring efforts on behalf of the people." Need I enforce this with any words of mine? It is a corollary from all that has been said here and elsewhere, and if you wish to have in a brief and condensed form the basis of our gratitude to him, here is the volume which I produce and make it appeal to you to adopt, with a unanimous voice, the proposition which reads as follows :—"That the Native community of Madras rejoice to feel that one of their fellow-countrymen is to have a seat in the British House of Commons—that they cordially congratulate Mr. Dadabhai Naoroji on being the first to win this proud distinction, and that they feel grateful to him for his unselfish and untiring efforts on behalf of the people of India." (Loud cheers.)

The Hon'ble Mr. V. Bashiam Aiyangar, in seconding the resolution, said :—

Mr. Chairman and Gentlemen,—I have great pleasure in rising to second the proposition which has been moved so ably by my friend, Mr. Ananda Charlu. The name of Mr. Dadabhai Naoroji has for years been a household word in every part of India with every educated native; and it is unnecessary, especially after the speech of Mr. Ananda Charlu, for me to refer to his various merits and excellent qualities. Mr. Dadabhai Naoroji is now three-score years of age; and the best part of his life, his talent, and his fortune have been devoted to the cause of his countrymen, and it is extremely gratifying that his unselfish and untiring efforts to serve his countrymen, by securing a seat in the British House of Commons, have at last been crowned with success. (Cheers.) He has for many years made the political and economic condition of India his study, and his knowledge of the various problems connected with the economic condition of India will prove eminently valuable in his career as a Member of Parliament, which, we all hope, may be a long one, and prove to be glorious and bright 'cheers, and be the means of securing representation of Indian people in the House of Commons, by one of their own countrymen ; and we may also hope that this will be a precursor of securing a representation in the Cabinet of one of the sons of India. '(Cheers.) Several years ago, it would have been hopeless to secure a seat in the House of Commons for a Native of India, and I believe that, although seven years ago, the result was by no means encouraging, but for the persevering and untiring efforts of Mr. Dadabhai Naoroji and the friends of India in England, he would not have made a second attempt.

Mr. P. R. Sundara Aiyar said :—

Mr. Chairman and Gentlemen,—I esteem it a great privilege to be allowed to support this proposition. Many people are surprised that Mr. Dadabhai Naoroji should have succeeded in winning the confidence and esteem of a British constituency ; but he had already succeeded in winning the admiration and the lasting affection of 250 millions of the people of India, of whom all but a handful of Parsees are as much aliens to him in race and religion as the electors of Central Finsbury. The fact is, gentlemen, Mr. Dadabhai Naoroji is no ordinary man. Recall to your mind the golden opinion he won as a student at school; his indefatigable industry, indomitable courage, unremitting perseverance, most earnest patriotism, and the sincerest love of duty throughout his long and distinguished career as a Professor of Mathematics in Elphinstone College, as an exponent of the views and aspirations of the Natives of India in all matters affecting this country, as a moderate and fearless critic of Government, as the Dewan of Baroda, as the trusted leader of the Congress party (cheers), as a useful and distinguished Member of the Bombay Legislative Council during the Viceroyalty of Lord Ripon, and the giant and victorious hero—or as Mr. Mehta called him the other day—the veritable hero of seven years' war. (Loud and prolonged cheering.) Recall to your mind also the inestimable service he rendered to us as the only native witness examined before the Parliamentary Com-

64

mittee. You cannot but come to the conclusion that Mr.
Dadabhai Naoroji was pre-eminently fitted to occupy the
proud and responsible position of the first Indian Member
for India. We may be indeed proud of Mr. Dadabhai
Naoroji. He has proved to conclusiveness that a "black
man" is fit to take part in the administration of the
Empire, whose territories are as wide as the known world.
He has made it impossible for interested persons to say
that Indians are unfit to take a substantial share in the
administration of their own country. It is a curious
coincidence that the election of Mr. Dadabhai Naoroji
should have closely followed the passing of the Indian
Councils Bill, which recognised the right of the people of
this country to take a substantial part in the proceedings
of their own deliberative assembly. These are events
which to my mind show that a bright day is dawning for the
country. It is impossible that it could be otherwise after
half a century of British rule, and after the mother of
Parliaments has recognised our rights to speak out our
grievances to her through the mouthpiece of her own representative. We hope that Mr. Dadabhai Naoroji's career
in Parliament may be a long and glorious one. (Cheers.)
We are confident that he will be a source of strength to
us in the House of Commons. We are also confident that
whatever may be the result of the scrutiny that is now
said to be going on with regard to his election as a member, if the electors of Central Finsbury are guided in the
future by the same feeling of sympathy with their voiceless
fellow-subjects in India, and if they are inspired by the
same unselfish generosity as they were inspired on this
occasion, they will find reason to repose in Mr. Dadabhai
Naoroji the same confidence that they have been able to
repose on the present occasion. (Cheers.)

The proposition and its object was explained in Tamil by
Mr. M. Viraraghava Chari, for the benefit of the merchant
classes which was strongly represented at the meeting.

The proposition was then carried amidst loud acclamation

It was proposed by Mr. M. O. Parthasarathy Aiyangar,
seconded by Mr. Cunniah Chetty, and carried, "That a
Committee, consisting of the Chairman and Mr. M.
Viraraghava Chari, be empowered to despatch at once
telegrams conveying the sense of resolution passed."

Mr. Viraraghava Chari at this stage read the following telegram from the President of the Nagercoil Club :— "Nagercoil Club joins Madras in congratulating Mr. Dadabhai Naoroji and the electors of Central Finsbury."

On the motion of Dr. Pulni Andy, seconded by Mr. C. Yethirajulu Naidu, a vote of thanks was passed to the Trustees of Pachaiyappah's Charities for lending the use of the Hall.

Another vote of thanks to the Chairman, proposed by Mr. Balajee Row, and seconded by Mr. Mahadeva Chetty, brought the meeting to a close.

Three cheers were called for the Electors of Central Finsbury, which were heartily responded to.

A CONGRATULATORY SONNET.

The following congratulatory sonnet, addressed to Dadabhai Naoroji, M.P., by R. Sivasankara Pandiyaji, B.A., F.T.S., was distributed at the meeting :—

> Dear Dadabhai Naoroji, good and great,
> Accept with kindness, patriot, true and bold,
> Defender firm of India, poor and old,
> A nation's thanks to thee, her advocate ;
> By facts and figures and by feats sedate
> At proper times with zeal then didst uphold,
> In England old, the cause of India now, behold !
> Now thy success she well doth celebrate.
> Although a hasty lord once blacken'd thee,
> Observant Finsbury yet makes thee shine
> Right well in Britain's Parliament supreme ;
> O Member of that body, fair and free,
> Just causes win at last ; may Sprite Divine
> Indeed bless thee with happiness extreme !

3. LORD HARRIS ON MR. NAOROJI.

At the annual evening party of the Gayan Samaj at Poona, Lord Harris exhorted the society to persevere and cultivate harmony and melody, pointing out the examples of the late Professor Apte and of Mr. Dadabhai Naoroji. He eulogised the deceased Professor for the remarkable success achieved by him in connexion with the Fergusson College. By their diligence and perseverance their example was an excellent instance of self-help. The return to Parliament of Mr. Dadabhai was pointed out as another signal and brilliant example of the same virtue. His

9

Excellency said he joined with the people of Bombay in their congratulations. With his party and as to political views he did not concern himself while he was in office in India, because he declined to admit that any of the great parties in England attempted to make capital out of Indian policy, but as a citizen of Bombay his lordship could identify himself with them, and as such he was proud that a Bombay native citizen should have been the first among the natives of India to enter Parliament. Mr. Dadabhai got there by confidence in himself and mainly by his own efforts; he fought not with one party but with both, and showed a wonderful example of perseverance and self-help.*

VI.

Congratulations in England.

1. MEETING OF THE INDIANS IN LONDON.

On Wednesday, June 20, a well-attended meeting of Indians residing in the United Kingdom was held at the National Liberal Club for the purpose of congratulating Mr. Dadabhai Naoroji on his election as a Member of Parliament, and thanking the electors of Central Finsbury for returning him. The Chair was taken by Rai Tej Narayan Singh, Bahadur. In opening the proceedings ·

The Chairman said :—

Ladies and Gentlemen,—Allow me to thank you for placing me in this position. It is an honour that I feel very deeply. I feel that I am unworthy to preside on such an occasion. I wish you could have had an able man—a recognised leader of the many millions of our country. This meeting represents all parts of India, and is thoroughly spontaneous in its character. We have met here to thank the electors of Central Finsbury—to express our deep gratitude to them. India rejoices at the fact that the British people are willing to recognise us as their fellow-subjects and fellow-citizens. The electors of Central Finsbury have given a proof of this by electing an Indian to a seat in the Imperial Parliament. Mr. Naoroji's

* Numerous other meetings have been held in various parts of India, not only in important towns, but also in minor localities, and even in hamlets and villages passing resolutions congratulating Mr. Dadabhai Naoroji and thanking the Finsbury electors; but for want of space we have to content ourselves with the principal ones.

election is unique in its kind. To India it is a great
honour. The history of England, as has been said, is a
chapter of romance. All honour to the electors of Central
Finsbury, for the credit is theirs! It is to thank them for
this ever-memorable election that we Hindoos, Mahom-
medans, Parsees, and Christians have met together to-day.
(Cheers.) With these words I will call upon Mr.
Mahmudal Huq (Mahomedan from Bengal) to move the
first resolution.

Mr. Mahmudal Huq :—

Mr. Chairman, Ladies, and Gentlemen,—It is the Briton's
boast to compare his Empire with that of the Romans, and
the pages of history fully justify, ay, more than justify,
that boast. Not only is this Empire larger than that
of the Romans, not only, like'the Romans, has he extended
gradually the same equitable laws, the same rights, the
same privileges which he enjoys to the inhabitants of
the conquered land, but he even takes into his bosom such
sons of the conquered land as he thinks fit for trust. Ay,
he goes further, he selects them to represent him in
the Imperial Parliament. Those noble Romans, whose
name even now we cannot mention without a feeling of
veneration, though centuries divide us from them, found
it very hard to concede this privilege to the conquered.
Their Imperial Senate, that majestic Senate of Rome,
thought an entrance within its walls to be a violation
of its sanctity. But what the noble Romans did not
do, the noble Briton has done. (Cheers.) What the
majestic Senate of Rome regarded as an intrusion, the still
more majestic and truly Imperial Senate of Great Britain,
the Imperial Parliament, regards as an additional welcome.
The election of Mr. Dadabhai Naoroji is a most remarkable
event, not only in the annals of British history, not only
in the annals of India, but, I may say, in the annals of
the world. It leaves a memorable landmark on the
history of Indian progress. But gentlemen, who are
they who thus enable the historian to embellish his
history with brilliant chapter? Who are they to whom
the credit is due? The electors of Central Finsbury.
It is they who have enabled us, through our distinguished
representative, Mr. Naoroji, to raise our voice in the Imperial Parliament on behalf of India. We know that
Mr. Naoroji is first an English member—he is Member

for the borough of Finsbury. It is not as an Indian that he takes his seat in Parliament ; he is Member for the borough of Finsbury, and as such, it will be his duty to look after the interests of that borough. No doubt, however, it is the duty of a British statesman, as it is the duty of all British politicians, to take an interest in Imperial and Colonial questions. Mr. Naoroji, owing to his vast Indian experience, will, no doubt, have a weight and authority in the House of Commons which an English member in a similar position would not be able to command. It is natural to expect that he will carry great weight there. But I am not sure whether in taking an interest in Indian questions, and devoting some portion of his time to them, he will not be serving the interests of British electors more than of Indians, because the British elector has a vast inheritance, a mighty British Empire to look after. It is the British elector who is chiefly responsible for the management of India. He is responsible in the eyes of God and in the eyes of mankind for the good management of India, and in taking an interest in Indian questions, Mr. Naoroji will be only doing his duty properly as a member for an English borough, and not as an Indian. It will no doubt be his duty—and no one knows it better than he does—to give attention to such questions as affect the British nation directly. I refer, for instance, to such questions as finance. I suppose I am not mistaken in saying that the one thing which the British taxpayer cares more for than another is the good management of finance. He always takes care to elect only such men as will keep a guardian eye over the finances of the country, because it directly affects his own purse. I am sure the electors of Central Finsbury may be congratulated on their choice, for they could not have had a more clear-headed or a sounder financier than Mr. Dadabhai Naoroji. (Cheers.) Before I move this resolution, I must thank the electors of Central Finsbury for showing a truly liberal spirit, a spirit that recognises no distinction of caste, colour, or creed. (Cheers.) We thank them for receiving us as brethren, not only theoretically but practically, for they have shown it, not only by words but by actions. The huzzahs of the multitude, the shouts of the people in India, point sufficiently to the fact that India regards with gratitude the action taken by the electors of Central Finsbury in having elected Mr. Naoroji to represent them in the Imperial Parliament. It is a remarkable fact which will not fail to arrest the attention of the historian. The event is one that will always be memorable in the annals of history, and posterity will look with admiring eyes upon it. What has happened in India itself ? All the cities are being illuminated, men of different views, men of different communities, are all uniting and vieing with each other in their expressions of gratitude to the electors of Central Finsbury, schools are closed, meetings are held, addresses are being poured forth, everything is being done to show the gratitude of the people to the electors of Central Finsbury. We Indians, residing in England, have only anticipated the formal thanks which are yet to come. We are nearer to Finsbury than they are, and can make our voice heard more easily. We have, therefore, held this meeting to thank the electors of Central Finsbury in our behalf, and not only in our behalf but in behalf of the great Indian nation. This fact is not without political significance. We regard it as a great political event. I am not going to discuss political questions, but I cannot help saying that if an Indian is fit to represent us in the Imperial Parliament, is it not time to consider whether Indians should not have greater power in the administration of their own country ? (Cheers.) The electors of Central Finsbury have sent us a message of good will. They regard our legitimate aspirations with great sympathy, and they have now given us a staff to lean upon. Even that is a great triumph for us, that our claims should have been so far recognised by the British people. Every lover of true human progress will admit that they have taken the first rank among the pioneers of reform. Their name will always be handed down to history as the enemies of prejudice and narrow-mindedness. I only hope that this trust which the electors have placed in Mr. Naoroji may long be in his hands, and that there may long exist the completest confidence between the electors and the elected. (Cheers.) I beg to move :—

"That this meeting of the inhabitants of India, at present residing in the United Kingdom, desires to express its heartfelt pleasure at the election of Mr. Dadabhai Naoroji as a member of the Imperial Parliament, which, it is aware, has given universal satisfaction throughout India, and it would take this opportunity of anticipating the voice of that great country by tendering its cordial thanks to the electors of Central Finsbury for choosing, as their representative in the House of Commons, one who commands the confidence and esteem of all classes of India."

Mr. J. C. Sarkar (Christian, from N. W. P.) :—

Mr. Chairman, Ladies, and Gentlemen,—The electors of Central Finsbury have within the last few days brought about an event which is likely to be one of the landmarks in the history of India, as well as the Parliamentary history of England. Its effects are likely to be far-reaching, and are likely to cause the name of Central Finsbury to be ever remembered with gratitude. I am not aware whether there ever was a native of another country elected as a member of the British Parliament ; but of this much I am certain, that no native of India ever before sat in that assembly as a member. (Hear, hear.) I hope this event marks the dawn of a new epoch, that more Indian members will be admitted into the British legislative chamber, and that it lays a substantial foundation of a real federation of a vast British Empire. The inhabitants of the Empire of India have ever been noted for their law-abiding instincts and loyalty to their sovereign, but probably at no time were the people of the whole of that country so devotedly loyal to one sovereign as they are this day to the throne of the good Queen and Empress who reigns over this Empire. (Cheers.) Her very name is cherished as that of a household goddess in millions of homes in India, and she is affectionately called the " *Empress-Mother*." But because the people of India are so loyal, it does not follow that they have no grievances, or that the present administration of India is perfect—a conclusion to which a large section of the British people have erroneously arrived. Far from it ; they have many grievances, and there are many defects in the administration. No foreigner, however well-informed he may be, can be so well fitted to fully set forth these grievances as a native of India who has personally experienced them, and who understands the feelings and wishes of the people, especially when that people have no voice of their own and are at such a distance. It is essentially necessary that this should be done, as continual silent suffering, ever so small, is likely to embitter the heart and cause despair. It is true we have in the House of Commons many members who are zealous, disinterested, and staunch friends of India, and whose good services to that country are invaluable ; yet Mr. Naoroji's case is very different, as he is an Indian, and his knowledge is derived from personal experience. We therefore rejoice, not only because a countryman of ours, who enjoys the universal confidence and respect of the people of India, has been thus honoured to a seat in the Imperial Legislature, but because an opportunity is thus afforded us of a direct channel by which the wants and wishes of the Indian people can be made known to the British nation and the Parliament. (Cheers.) I have no doubt that the electors of Central Finsbury will find in Mr. Naoroji an honest, conscientious, painstaking, and able representative, and that their interest will never suffer in his hands. As far as India is concerned, perhaps no one man could have been elected who enjoys so much the confidence of all classes of its people. Mr. Naoroji's knowledge of statistics, his skill in debate, and his capacity for business, fit him peculiarly to act as the representative of a class or classes of men. Some people have lately said that Mr. Naoroji, so far as his Indian representative character is concerned, represents only a small class of the Indian community, and not the whole country. This is a groundless assertion. If Mr. De Courcey, a descendant of the Normans, who came to England some centuries ago, and who is a Roman Catholic by religion, can be a representative of the Saxons, the Scotch, the Irish, &c., who are settled in a certain borough, and who profess religions as divergent from Roman Catholicism as Hinduism is from Mohammedanism, surely Mr. Naoroji can represent the people of India, where his forefathers settled thirteen hundred years ago. But the word " representation " is often misinterpreted, for the purpose of telling the people of India that it is impossible for them to find any man, or set of men, who·can be said to be their representatives. A slight consideration will show that in that strict literal sense, representation of one man for all the dwellers of a city or borough would be impossible in any country in the world. The people of India have ever been undemonstrative, and yet this event of Mr. Naoroji's election has caused so much excitement in India as has seldom been seen before. On receipt of the news schools were closed, houses and streets were illuminated, innumerable telegrams of congratulation were wired, and general rejoicings

took place. Even the ruling princes of India have gone
out of their usual course, and sent telegrams to Mr.
Naoroji, and otherwise expressed their pleasure in more
substantial ways. All this indisputably proves that Mr.
Naoroji's election has caused universal satisfaction in
India, and that he fully possesses the confidence and
esteem not only of its people, but of its ruling princes also.
It is a notorious fact that India and its concerns are very
little cared for by the generality of the members of the
House of Commons. The introduction of an Indian question, including such important business as the dicussion
of the Budget, which affects the weal or woe of millions
of Her Majesty's subjects, ever acts as a dinner bell to the
member of the House, and these momentous questions are
discussed by no more than half-a-dozen members in an
empty house. Therefore, the election of a native of India,
though as a representative of an English borough, is a
distinct gain to India, for which our sincere and heartfelt
thanks are due to the electors of Central Finsbury, who
have so bravely broken through the ordinary practice of
the country, and elected an Indian as their representative
in their national assembly, thereby extending the hand
of fellowship and uniting themselves in the close bonds of
friendship with the two hundred and eighty millions of
their fellow-subjects in the distant Indian Empire. With
these few remarks I beg to second the resolution submitted
to you for adoption. (Cheers.)

Mr. T. M. Nair (Hindu, Madras) :—

Mr. Chairman, Ladies, and Gentlemen,—After the
eloquent and exhaustive speeches of the proposer and
seconder of the resolution, there is left but little for
me to say. I cannot, however, refrain from saying a
few words on this occasion as the representative of
Indian students residing in Scotland. I am particularly glad to have this opportunity of speaking to-day
because my presence here may prove, in some respects at least, that complete co-operation and harmony
exist between Indians residing in different parts of the
United Kingdom. You may also be pleased to learn that
we are anxious on this occasion, as well as on every other
occasion, to prove that those Indians who have' found a
temporary home north of the Tweed are not behind their
countrymen residing in London, or anywhere else, in

appreciating the significance and importance of the brilliant event which is to make India's voice heard in the British House of Commons a few days hence. (Gentlemen, it is not necessary for me to go into any details as to Mr. Naoroji's qualifications to represent Indian public opinion in Parliament. If I were speaking to a British audience, it might, perhaps, be necessary to go into these details; but in a meeting like this, composed almost entirely of Indians there can only be one prevailing sentiment—that is a sentiment of confidence, respect, and love towards the veteran financier and statesman of India. (Cheers.) We know what Mr. Naoroji's worth is, and we have always respected him accordingly. It is still more gratifying to us to find that people in Great Britain, too, have recognised his worth. I cannot help recalling some few incidents. The other day, when standing in front of *The Scottish Leader* office when the result of his election was announced, there was a ringing cheer sent up by the crowd that was waiting for the announcement. Again, at the great meeting at West Calder, when Mr. Gladstone incidentally mentioned Mr. Naoroji's name, it created such enthusiasm as ought to make any Indian proud of his countryman. (Cheers.) We cannot forget that we owe all this to the electors of Central Finsbury, who, against powerful influences that have been brought to bear, and to which, perhaps, I need not allude here, have set an example for other British constituencies to follow. It is only meet and proper, therefore, that we should offer our hearty thanks to those electors, and it is for that reason that I have great pleasure in supporting this proposal. I wish before I sit down to say a few words as a matter of apology from some of my friends in Edinburgh. Perhaps they would have taken a greater share in this meeting but for some slight misunderstanding. A notice was sent to us announcing that an address was to be presented to Mr. Naoroji by Indians residing in England, and we naturally thought that, not being resident in England, we should not be able to participate in it; and we therefore thought of preparing another address for ourselves. Since the phrase has been altered from "residing in England" to "residing in the United Kingdom," we have been glad heartily to join in this matter. We have been told that England here in London represents Scotland as well as England, but north of the Tweed we do not recognise any such thing; we still

10

hold that Scotland is different from England, and hence I hope you will excuse the misunderstanding.

Mr. Jaishi Ram (Hindu, Bengal):—

Mr. Chairman, Ladies and Gentlemen,—This is a most auspicious occasion, meeting, as we do, to perform the pleasant duty of thanking and congratulating the electors of Central Finsbury for returning Mr. Dadabhai Naoroji as a Member of Parliament. Gentlemen, the electors of Central Finsbury have had a hard fight. While working in the office of Mr. Naoroji during the times of the election, I noticed the display of the greatest enthusiasm, zeal, and earnestness on the part of the electors, and I think, therefore, they are deserving of every credit. They have solved that great problem which the Prime Minister, the political rival of the so-called Grand Old Man, and the Leader of the Conservative party, declared a few years ago to be absurd and impracticable. The sensation which was at that time created must be fresh in your minds. The thanks of the Indian public as well as of the British are due to the electors of Central Finsbury, who have not only succeeded in removing the impression then created, but have done much to establish mutual confidence between two different races. (Cheers.) The connection between India and England is no less valuable to the one than it is to the other. Is the administration of India perfect? What do we see here? Ireland contains only five million people, and one-third of the time of Parliament is devoted to Irish affairs. India—I may say poor India —has a population of 250,000,000 and the hours occupied in considering its affairs in Parliament may be counted on the fingers. This is a great neglect on the part of the House of Commons so far as India is concerned. What are the feelings of the Indians with regard to this neglect? I read this in a paper received by the last mail representing the views of the North-West Frontier of British India—I mean *The Tribune :* "When the late Mr. George Yule said at the fourth Indian National Congress that the House of Commons had thrown back the trust upon Providence in respect of the responsibility of the Indian Government, he stated less than the fact. What are we to think of the news that the Indian Budget statement in the House of Commons was listened to by only six

Members ? Even the fact that Parliament is on the eve of dissolution can be no justification for such a culpable neglect of Indian affairs. It is a standing complaint that the Indian Budget is introduced towards the fag-end of the session, but beyond a casual and feeble protest now and then nothing has been done by the members themselves to remedy this grievance." This is not the view of the English public generally; but those Englishmen who are acquainted with the affairs of India concur in it. In the *Statesman* of the 18th of June I read :—" Mr. Jeremiah Lion, of London, who is well-known to the commercial community of India, has written the following letter to a native gentleman in this city :—' I thank you for your good wishes on my candidature. A powerful factor in determining me to accept this honourable position was that I might raise my voice on behalf of my fellow British subjects in India. At present India is treated like a poor relation. We introduce her to Parliament at the fag-end of the session, when no one stays to listen to her claims. Like our poor in our East-end slums are neglected by the wealthier residents in the West-end of London, similarly is India treated with contemptuous indifference.' " This, Sir, is the complaint of India, but it is expected that through the presence of Mr. Naoroji in the House of Commons such a state of things will not long exist. It is hoped that in consequence of his presence the members will be more attentive and more earnest and dutiful towards the millions of India. I beg to support the resolution. (Cheers.)

Mr. J. Ghose (of Calcutta) :—

Mr. President and Gentlemen,—When I entered this room I had no intention of addressing this meeting, but, being an Indian, I feel so stirred by what has been said by previous speakers that I cannot help adding a few words that I think have been left unsaid by them. We Indians cannot be sufficiently grateful to England for all that we have got. No other nation could have given us so much. What we have received, however, in the past has been from particular Governments or from Members of Parliament; but the present occasion of rejoicing we owe to the English people. (Cheers.) If we can once touch the hearts of the English people our days will be as bright as those of any other nation. What we want is to get a true feeling of sympathy and good will from our British fellow-subjects; and the electors of Central Finsbury have shown that if we will but appear before them in the right way they will be only too ready to help us. Others will do the same, but to them belongs the credit of taking the first step, of taking us by the hand and sending our friend Mr. Naoroji to the House of Commons, not in our interest alone, but in theirs. (Cheers.) And what greater proof of confidence can there be than this? Then let me say that those who allege that Mr. Naoroji is a Parsee, and does not represent Indians, are greatly mistaken. In England itself, if a person is a Jew, like the late Lord Beaconsfield, or a Roman Catholic, it matters not; he resides in England, and his interests are identical with those of his fellow-countrymen, and that is sufficient to make him an Englishman. So it is with Mr. Naoroji. His interests are identical with those of Hindus; and why should not Hindus, Mohammedans, and all other religions rejoice when they see this Parsee gentleman in the House of Commons representing the cause of India? (Hear, hear.) Those who think that the present race of educated Hindus are disloyal are greatly mistaken; in fact, I should say that they are behind the age in point of intelligence. Does education make one more or less capable of understanding one's advantages? There can be no two answers to this. An educated Indian knows his interests much better than an uneducated Indian; and the education which an Indian gets, and which he completes in England, cannot tell him that it will be to the advantage of his country to be separated from England, and to lose the advantage of its strength. He may say that India under the Indians would be more powerful than she is at present, and that she would make more progress. But have we not now all that Englishmen have achieved during the last two thousand years ready at our door, all their civilisation, all their education, all their improvement; and are we to throw this away, and begin to work anew with all the disabilities that lie in our way as Indians living in a hot climate? The poor and uneducated are not so well able to understand their interests as the educated. When the mutiny of 1857 took place, who were the persons who rose against the English Government? Not the educated, but the uneducated. The more one sees what progress India has made during the last hundred years or so, the more one feels a love for that Government, the more one feels that he is himself a part of the English people. Though he may not be of the same colour, and may not enjoy all the benefits of the English climate, he has English literature, and what can he desire more? If all the things of this earth were taken from me I should not begrudge them, so long as Shakespeare and Milton were left me. (Cheers.) I have much pleasure in supporting the resolution.

Mr. P. C. Roy (Bengal Civil Service) :—

After the brilliant speeches which we have heard, I feel somewhat nervous in addressing so large a gathering; but as the sentiment which has been evoked by the election of Mr. Naoroji has been so deep and universal, I think each of us should endeavour to express his views on the subject. We all in England rejoice that Mr. Naoroji has been returned to Parliament, and we come here to congratulate him, and to thank the electors of Central Finsbury for electing him. What is the reason of our rejoicing? That question has been ably answered by some of my predecessors. Hitherto we have not had in the British House of Commons a single representative. Every other part of the Empire which is not a self-governing colony has its representative there except India; and it is not, therefore, surprising to find that on the first occasion when an Indian has been elected, all India should unite in celebrating the event with due *éclat*. (Cheers.) And this sentiment is not confined to the educated classes. I beg to differ slightly in this respect from the last speaker. The sentiment is universal. Every man in India who understands what his interests are, who feels the burden of the salt tax or any other grievance that weighs upon him, will learn with great joy and gratification the news that one of their own countrymen has been elected to the Parliament which legislates for the whole British Empire. (Cheers.) What is Mr. Naoroji's position in India that we consider him to be so fit a person to represent us in the British Parliament? There may be some here of various political views, but I am sure that every Conservative, as well as every Liberal, will admit that Mr. Naoroji is the Grand Old Man of India; that he is one of our foremost men. He is regarded by the advanced Liberal section of the Indian community to be *the* patriot, the one unassuming, sincere, and thoroughly honest worker among the Indian people. Even those who do not think with him in political matters—though I believe they are in a minority—entertain the sincerest veneration for the name of Dadabhai Naoroji. It is not surprising, therefore, that all India should unite, as it does, in celebrating this occasion. It is a precedent which I am sure will be followed on other occasions. I sincerely trust that Mr. Naoroji will not be the only Indian elected to the House of Commons. I trust also that the time is not far distant when the people of India will have some voice in the government of their own country. The system under which India is at present ruled is an anomaly in a country like England, where every man breathes the air of freedom. Even we who come from a distant country feel, the moment we are on English soil, that our chains fall from us, and that we breathe an atmosphere of freedom that we do not breathe in the land of our birth. I am very sorry to be at all excited, but I think that all my fellow-countrymen who are present will echo the sentiments that I have expressed. We are taunted with the fact that there is no unity in India, no Indian nation. It is true that we are of different races and religions and languages. But what constitutes the idea of nationality in the present day? Is it unity of language? Is it unity of race? Is it unity on any other condition than that of perfect unity in thought and political sentiment? What do you call the United States but a nation? Yet look at its component parts. Does it not largely consist in many states of Italians speaking the Italian language, in others of Germans speaking the German language, in others of Frenchmen speaking the French? Yet they are all united in one nation. Take Hungary again. But I need not multiply instances to show that difference of race, of language, and religion is no bar to perfect political unity. (Cheers.) I am sure we are all prepared to admit that we owe it to British rule that we are at the present day more or less united in India. I do not say that it would have occurred without British rule. Even Englishmen who desire to retain their Empire in India cannot conceal from themselves the obvious fact that there is growing up in India a unity which is the direct consequence of their own rule. (Cheers.) And it cannot be faced by any other means than by recognising the importance of the Indian people in the British Empire, and frankly admitting them to the rights and privileges which Englishmen have themselves acquired after long and arduous fighting. (Cheers.)

On the motion of Mr. J. N. Ray, seconded by Mr. Tarrachand, a vote of thanks was passed to the Chairman for presiding, and the proceedings then terminated.

---

2. BANQUET AT THE HOLBORN RESTAURANT.

A complimentary dinner was given on Saturday, July 23, at the Holborn Restaurant to Mr. Dadabhai Naoroji, M.P., in celebration of his election as Member for Central Finsbury. The company included about a hundred and thirty inhabitants of India, among whom were eight or nine ladies. Mr. M. M. Bhownaggree, c.i.e., occupied the chair, and he was supported by Mr. P. C. Roy, Mr. T. M. Nair, Mahmoodul Hug, Rai Tej Narayan Singh Bahadur, Mr. and Mrs. Tarachand, Mr. N. J. Moolla, Mr. and Miss Sarkar, Dr. Miss Cama, Mrs. Pherose Thomas, Mr. D. J. Tata, Mr. J. D. Cola, Bai Rukhmabai, Mr. A. S. M. Ziaur Rahman, Miss C. J. Sorabji, Miss Vakeel, Mahmood Ali Khan, Mr. K. S. Bonnerjee, &c. The following telegram was received from Mr. Wm. Digby, c.i.e. :—" Deeply regret serious illness in my family makes it impossible for me to be present this evening. Kindly convey to Mr. Dadabhai and to the meeting this expression of regret, and to your guest my hearty congratulations on his election as Member for Central Finsbury."

After dinner, the Chairman said :—

Ladies and gentlemen,—The first toast which I have the honour and privilege of proposing is that of Her Majesty the Queen of England and Empress of India. (Cheers.) This toast is usually received in all countries under the Empire of Great Britain with much enthusiasm, but there is no part of the world under the British sovereignty where it is received with greater enthusiasm or with more loyal feelings than it is in all parts of India. (Cheers.) Her Majesty has, throughout a long and beneficent reign, extending over more than half a century, shown on various occasions and by various means in her power, and by acts of kindness to populations as well as to individuals, her great interest in her Empire of India. (Cheers.) The Victorian age is distinguished for many historical events. India has known many acts of benevolent government during that period, and it is a matter of supreme satisfaction that in Her Majesty's reign the great historical event which we are met to-night to celebrate has occurred. (Cheers.) I am perfectly sure that throughout the length and breadth of the British dominions there is no one who will hear with greater satisfaction than herself of that pæan of praise and love and affection towards the British Crown which the election of Mr. Dadabhai Naoroji to Parliament has evoked. (Loud cheers.) I give you " The Health of Her Most Gracious Majesty Queen Victoria, Empress of India."

The toast was drunk with great enthusiasm.

The Chairman :—

Ladies and gentlemen,—The next toast which I have the honour to propose, and for which I anticipate as cordial a reception as that given to the toast of the Queen, is " The Prince and Princess of Wales and the rest of the Royal Family." (Cheers.) The Prince and Princess of Wales have ever taken a keen interest in matters relating to India ; and His Royal Highness made himself beloved by high and low alike throughout India when he visited that country. The sympathy evoked in every part of the Indian empire by the great loss which the Prince and Princess of Wales recently suffered testifies to the great love in which they are held there. In a greater or less degree the same may be said of the other members of the Royal Family. But there is one name which, in an assembly like this, I should single out for special mention : I mean the Duke of Connaught, as well as his august consort. (Cheers.) In more than one part of India their Royal Highnesses, in the course of their residence during a long period, by personal intercourse with different communities, made themselves beloved and respected ; and I believe I am only uttering the wish that is generally entertained in India in this connection when I express the hope that His Royal Highness may again, at an early opportunity, go to reside among them in a high official capacity. (Cheers.)

The toast was duly honoured.

Rai Tej Narayan Singh Bahadur :—

Mr. Chairman, ladies, and gentlemen,—I have great pleasure in proposing the toast, " The Viceroy and

Governor-General of India, the representative of Her Majesty the Queen-Empress." (Cheers.) We are extremely fortunate in having the noblest sons of England sent out to our country to rule over our destinies. The position of Governor-General and Viceroy of India is a most responsible one, and the difficulties with which he has to contend are enormous. I request you to drink the health of Lord Lansdowne, the present Viceroy. (Cheers.)

The Chairman :—

Ladies and gentlemen,—It is now my pleasing duty to give you the toast of the evening, the health of Mr. Dadabhai Naoroji—(loud and prolonged cheering) the Member for Central Finsbury. Before I proceed further, I will call upon the Secretary of the Organising Committee of this banquet to read an address which has been prepared on behalf of those who have joined it—namely, all those inhabitants of India who happen to be within visiting range of this place.

Rai Narayan Singh Bahadur read the following address :—

To DADABHAI NAOROJI, ESQ.,

Member of Parliament for the Central Division of the Metropolitan Borough of Finsbury.

" Sir,—We, the Indians residing in the United Kingdom, desire to express our joy at your election as the Representative of the Central Division of Finsbury to the Imperial Parliament.

" We do not think it necessary on this occasion to enter into any details of all your long and arduous services to our Mother-country, beyond stating that all classes of the Indian people—Hindus, Mahomedans, Parsees, and others—have their entire confidence in you as fit to represent fairly and fully their wants and wishes to the British Public.

" Our chief desire on this occasion is to put on record our deep debt of gratitude and our thankfulness to the electors of Central Finsbury for returning you as their Representative to the House of Commons, and to all other ladies and gentlemen who have assisted in the work. We are sure, Sir, from our knowledge of your past life and record, that you will serve your Constituency faithfully and well and

11

give to it every satisfaction. But while thus doing your duty to your Constituency, we rejoice that India will now have the opportunity of having her cause pleaded before the great British People and Parliament by one of her own sons from her own point of view.

"We are not insensible of our obligations to several English gentlemen, notably persons like Bright, Fawcett, Bradlaugh and others, who have raised their voice from time to time on our behalf; but we cannot help hoping that the voice of one of ourselves, and in whom we have such full confidence, will be listened to with generosity and indulgence.

"By your election, Sir, we have one more signal proof of the desire of the British people to govern India with justice and to promote her welfare, and such proofs cannot but strengthen largely the already existing loyalty and attachment of the Indian People to the British Crown. Your election is a great event in the Annals of India, and, we venture to say, in the Annals of the British Empire.

"We repeat, Sir, that we rejoice in this event, and we wish you a long life of future usefulness, and happiness to yourself." (Loud cheers.)

Mr. Nair read a similar address prepared by Indians residing in Scotland.

The Chairman :—

I have just received from the Secretary to the Indian Association in Edinburgh this telegram :—" Chairman, Indian Dinner, Holborn Restaurant. Enthusiastic meeting Indian Association wishes success to the unique assembly unprecedented in the annals of history." (Cheers.) Mr. Dadabhai Naoroji, in handing you these addresses, I beg to call your attention to the fact that around you are gathered at this festive board men from all parts and communities of India to celebrate your return to the British Parliament by the constituents of Central Finsbury, an historical event which rises above the level of party politics. (Loud cheers.) There have been empires in the world from a remote period in its history, which have held dependencies and established colonies, and it has been the aim of the wisest among the statesmen of those empires to give preferment to places of power and position to men of those nations that owed them allegiance. It is true that they partly succeeded. The Romans, for

example, had their Nubian kings. But we all know as a
matter of history that the exigencies of administration
have always placed restraints upon the fulfilment and con-
summation of such an aim; till, coming to the present
time, we find that it had been reserved for the English
nation to find a way through those barriers, and for a part
of that nation to adopt as their representative in their
own Parliament a fellow-subject from one of the dependencies of the empire—one whom by birth and nurture
India is proud to claim as one of her most illustrious sons.
(Cheers.) It is true that it has fallen to the lot of the
Liberal party, and the electors of Central Finsbury, to
perform this notable act which will live for many a genera-
tion to come in the grateful recollection of the people of
India. But let it be calmly considered and remembered
that at the back of the franchise so nobly exercised is the
grand constitution of Great Britain, which, regardless of
politics or parties, steadily moves on its course of freedom
from principle to principle. (Cheers.) And let me
venture to express on your behalf a hope that the day is
not far distant when our friends on the Conservative side
may find a fellow-subject from India of their own way of
thinking, and see fit to elect him as a representative of
one of their own constituencies in the British Parliament.
(Cheers.) That is now only a matter of time, and is
certainly within the range of practical politics, and I
would fain hope, for the sake of the union of England and
India—their everlasting union—that it may soon come to
pass, so that not only one party, or one constituency, but
the British nation as a whole may show to the world that
they are proud to regard their fellow-subjects in India as
common citizens under one crown and one empire.
(Applause.) In saying this I am sure I only express your
sentiment that it is no mere political or party act which
we are celebrating to-night, but that it is an essentially
patriotic act on the part of the electors of Central Finsbury we rejoice at, its patriotism consisting in this—that
rising above considerations of party or politics, it recognises that the British Empire embraces in its fold of loyal
devotion to Her Majesty's person and rule the millions of
their Indian fellow-subjects whom the electors of Central
Finsbury regard as fit for the enjoyment of equal rights
with themselves. (Cheers.) Coming now ·to speak of
the eminent person who has been fortunate enough to

bring about this great event, I will ask you to bear with me for a few moments while I recall to remembrance a few of the prominent acts of his life. They are matter of history, and written in biographies over and over again. But India is a large continent of diverse peoples, and you who come from so many different parts of it may well be asked to listen for a few moments to those eventful acts in the career of the honourable guest of the evening, so that our feelings of gratitude towards him may be keener if possible, and our admiration for him intensified. Mr. Naoroji was a most distinguished and promising student among the first batch of those of our countrymen who were educated in the Elphinstone Institution; and even from early life he began to fulfil the ample promise which he gave in his student days, by being appointed to the post of professor in the same institution in which he had been taught. He became there a leader of a band remembered to-day with feeling of gratitude throughout India, more especially in Bombay, and for nothing so much as for their efforts to ameliorate the condition of their womankind. That itself was a happy augury for men who aimed at raising the standard of enlightenment among their countrymen. Such persons were necessarily capable of great things. They knew that by educating their womankind, by making intelligent and good mothers of them, they would raise up a race of men who would be competent to wield, by-and-by, the affairs of their own provinces and of their own country. (Cheers.) To this interesting and philanthropic work Mr. Dadabhai Naoroji devoted a great many valuable days, and much of his then slender resources, and 1 can testify as one who has known something of the conditions of female education in India, that although it has progressed since that period by rapid strides, the initial efforts put forward under the guidance of Mr. Dadabhai Naoroji are still remembered with lively feelings of gratitude in Bombay, I may say throughout India. (Cheers.) I believe it was from the Elphinstone Institution, after having for some years worked for the good of his countrymen and countrywomen in various capacities, that Mr. Dadabhai Naoroji got an opportunity of coming to England; and it was an auspicious coming. He came in connection with a mercantile firm, and before long founded one for himself; and it is to prove his great desire to advance the interest of his fellow-

countrymen that I recall here the fact of his having attempted to get from India all the co-operation which in
his mercantile affairs he needed. He would have got
that assistance here on easier terms, but he thought that
by some self-sacrifice he could put profitable opportunities
in the way of some of the educated young men of his
country by calling them here, and there are many instances
of persons who even at this day remember his invitation to
them with the deepest gratitude. That was the beginning
of that colony of Indians in England which we see so
numerously and intelligently represented at this table.
I must again take you back a little to one or two other
notable acts of his performed in earlier life in Bombay before
he came to England. The most significant of them was
the establishment of, I believe, the first vernacular journal
in Bombay, the *Ras Goftar*, and side by side with it the
establishment of a journal for the promotion of education
among females, named *Sri Bodh*. He also founded the
"Society for the Promotion of Knowledge." These are
works which must not be forgotten, because these journals
and the Society from the first successfully tried to do what
they are still vigorously doing, and what ·I hope they
will continue to do for many long years to come,
namely, promote enlightenment and knowledge among
an important section of the native community of
India. (Cheers.) After coming to England, although
Mr. Naoroji became a successful merchant, he was
never very rich; but I may mention here, as an example of his charitable instincts, what is not very widely
known and what I am announcing publicly perhaps for the
first time, that at a time when he was not wealthy in the
ordinary sense of the word, he offered to the Government
of India 50,000 rupees out of his own pocket to establish,
in connection with some of his countrymen, scholarships
for enabling promising native students to study in England.
(Cheers.) That scheme, unfortunately, was never brought
to fulfilment ; but it is worthy of record, as an instance of
the quiet spirit of benevolence which Mr. Naoroji has
always entertained towards his country, and which he has
tried to manifest in more ways than one. Another *rôle*
which Mr. Dadabhai Naoroji filled was that of a religious
reformer. He was the founder, or one of the founders, of
what is to-day a well-known society for the reform of the
Zoroastrian religion. Although that society appeals only

to a section of the Indian populations, still I recal the fact to show that wherever there was room for reform and progress, he made the breach and invaded at all points ; and you may well imagine that he lived laborious days and almost sleepless nights in that effort. In various capacities and in various directions he led the van of reform, whether it related to his own race, or to the people of India generally. (Cheers. During his further residence in England, he again devoted a large portion of his time to public matters for the good of India. One of the prominent things that he did was to establish the East India Association, which has been in the past more, I am sorry to say, than in the present, a means of diffusing a correct knowledge and a true representation of the sentiments of the different parts of India among the public in London and throughout England. By means of the agency of that association, as well as in various other ways—such as correspondence with the Secretary of State and other officials responsible for the government of India—he sought to secure for our countrymen further rights and privileges and larger employment in the public service ; and he altogether worked for a better acquaintance on the part of the English with the wants of India. From his career in England he was, after some years, called upon to undertake a very responsible, I may say the most responsible, post that could at that period be entrusted to any one in connection with a native state of India, I mean that of Prime Minister of Baroda. Baroda was in an almost helpless condition at the time when the co-operation of Mr. Dadabhai Naoroji was invited. He willingly went there, more from patriotic than from personal motives, because he had always been a great friend of the native states of India. He wanted to increase its prosperity, after securing it from an impending peril, and to show what educated Indians placed in responsible positions were capable of in the way of governing important portions of their own country. (Cheers.) I could tell many an interesting tale of the eventful career of Mr. Naoroji in this capacity, of the war that he waged with contending elements, and of the successes he achieved. But ultimately events so combined that he had to resign his post—not, however, before he had accomplished some notable improvements, the traces of which are to be found up to the present day. (Cheers.) That, gentlemen, is an acknowledged fact in current history. None but those

who are unaware of the condition of affairs at that time
can controvert the statement I have made ; and it is therefore pleasing to learn that among the best friends of Mr.
Dadabhai Naoroji at the present moment, and foremost
among those who have signified their satisfaction at the
great success which he has achieved, is the reigning illustrious Gaekwar of Baroda himself. (Cheers.) This reference to Baroda reminds me of what, perhaps, is not very
publicly known here, or at least what has been in some
quarters disputed—that as of the people so of the princes,
Mr. Dadabhai Naoroji is a truthful, a competent, and an
accepted representative. (Cheers.) Princes and persons
may differ from him in details of opinions and sentiments; but I do not believe that there is any body
of men, or any man of note, much less a prince, who
will say that in representing the aspirations of the
Indian communities, in advocating the rights of princes and
peoples alike, Mr. Dadabhai Naoroji is not truly representing the prevailing feeling throughout all India. I will not
detain you with any detailed description of the other more
recent acts performed by him in his capacity as a member
of the Bombay Municipality, or as a member of the Council
of the Governor of Bombay. But I may sum up briefly
that in all the positions to which either the Government or
the people have preferred him, he has honestly, conscientiously, and to the entire approval both of the classes and
the masses, discharged those functions that have fallen to
his lot. Throughout all his long and eventful life there
have been many eminent qualities of the head, as well as
of the heart, that have marked his varied career. His
moderation has been proverbial, and I believe I may claim
for·him the credit that he has no enemy. His temperance
of language, even when engaged in debates and discussions
of a warm nature, has been remarkable, and may well give
to us and to others of his countrymen an example which
we might do well to follow.—Mr. Dadabhai Naoroji, you
have, through various stages of an eventful life,

"Moving up from high to higher,
Become on Fortune's crowning slope,
The pillar of a people's hope,
The centre of a world's desire." (Cheers.)

This sir, I assure you, is no mere figure of speech. It
is true in every word and every letter of it. The reliance
of the people of India on your advocacy is a well-known

fact. The conscientious and ample way in which you have discharged those functions which have been entrusted to you by the common voice of the people is now an accepted matter broadly recognised. You have, more than any other man in India, I venture to say become the anchor of their aspirations. And in concluding this feeble speech in support of the toast of the evening, let me, on behalf of all our friends here, and on behalf of all India from every part of which these friends come, express the hope that you may, by the grace of God, be enabled to discharge your new trust in the British House of Parliament, to the entire approval of your own conscience, which means the satisfaction of the vast population of India, and that you may be granted a long, healthy, and prosperous life to fulfil its responsible duties. (Loud and prolonged cheers.)

Mr. Dadabhai Naoroji (who was received with enthusiastic and prolonged cheering) said :—

Mr. Chairman, Ladies and Gentlemen,—I really do not know what words to use to express the deep feeling in my heart for the extraordinarily cordial and kind manner in which you have received this toast. The occasion on which I am standing before you is, as has been often expressed, a most eventful one; and, apart from my own personality, I echo the first words of the address and participate in the joy which you feel. It is an event of the greatest moment to India that an English constituency has been liberal enough to hold forth its hand to a fellow-subject from India to enable him to go and represent the wants and wishes of his country before the Imperial Parliament. (Cheers.) For this reason I participate in the joy which you evince so cordially and enthusiastically. Many words have been said this evening about myself, and the two addresses also speak very kindly of me. The Chairman has been pleased to speak in too flattering terms of my past career. ("No, no.") All I can say at present is that I have simply tried to do that duty which my English education taught me both towards my country and my rulers; and why I did my duty towards my rulers was because I was convinced that we had a nation ruling over us whose fundamental idea of rule was based on justice and the welfare of the people. (Cheers.) Forty years ago when I made my first political speech, at the inauguration of the Bombay Association, I expressed this sentiment, that we need no other means by which to make our rulers listen to our wants or our views, and redress any wrongs that we may complain of, beyond constitutionally representing our wishes to them; and that I was quite sure that whenever we were just in our aspirations and our demands, the very instinct of the British people would compel them to grant them. Such was the sentiment that I expressed forty years ago; and to my entire satisfaction I stand here to-day in the due and complete fulfilment of the idea that I have so long cherished. (Cheers.) It has been the secret of my strength that I have always, without any hesitation or flinching, continued to work in my way unceasingly without any fear, because I had this one strong conviction in my mind, that, whatever may happen, when once the British public are satisfied as to the justice of any demand that I or my countrymen may make, we are sure in the end to obtain it. (Cheers.) I have worked on these lines, and I think I have been correct in doing so. The event of this day, which you have met together to celebrate, most signally and emphatically proves the truth of the sentiment on which I have acted during all this period. It is no small event that a British constituency should accept an Indian fellow-subject as their representative, with confidence that he would do his duty towards them, while at the same time he would be enabled to give utterance to the voice of his countrymen, comprising hundreds of millions of their fellow-citizens. That is the sentiment that has largely influenced the electors of Central Finsbury, who are justly entitled to whatever thanks you may give to them. Taking that as an instance of the good will and sincerity of the British public in treating India fairly as a portion of the British Empire, there is one feature in it to which I want particularly to draw your attention. That the people in India and we here should be overjoyed at this event is only natural. It is a great step in our political advancement; but the feature that I want to allude to is this, that if one were to judge from the numbers of telegrams and letters that I receive from English ladies and gentlemen in different parts of the United Kingdom, one would suppose that the English people were rejoicing over something that had happened to themselves. (Cheers.) These letters and telegrams are full of expressions of joy, and the reason is

12

very simple. They now feel satisfied that whatever they
had professed in former days as to their desire to treat
India justly and generously, it has been signally fulfilled
by this one act. They naturally, therefore, rejoice that the
electors of Central Finsbury should have given a distinct
proof of the real desire and wishes of the British public. I
will not enter largely into the question of the benefits that
we receive from British rule. It is a long history. The
very fact that we are met together here, speaking different
languages—one half not being able to understand the
other half if they spoke in the vernacular—and that we
are expressing in one and the same language, the language
of our rulers, our joy on this occasion, is in itself the best
proof of the great benefit that England has bestowed upon
India. (Cheers.) As another proof on a larger scale,
though we may not all agree with the views of the
National Congress, I may instance it as a phenomenon of
a most significant character. Such a thing as the Indian
National Congress never existed in the annals of Indian
history, because it could not under the circumstances in
which the Indian people were living. They were people
having different languages and different religions, and the
whole of India was broken up into many different king-
doms. There was no common language and no common
means of journeying over the whole country. To-day they
meet Hindoos, Mohammedans, Parsees, and Christians all
meeting at one spot, having travelled thousands of miles and
expressing their sentiments towards their British rulers, and
uttering their complaints freely and outspokenly. This is a
phenomenon which would have been utterly impossible except
under the *régime* which the British Government has established. The education we have received, the freedom of
speech which we are enjoying, the liberty, and sometimes the
warmth, with which we speak of our grievances towards
our rulers—all this shows that we are under a rule which
is benignant, and which really and sincerely desires our
good. I need not further enlarge on this topic, because
every one of us, especially those who have received an
English education and are imbued with English literature
and English politics, understands and appreciates the
benefits we have received from British rule. But there
are certain circumstances which require a clear exposition
before the British public and the British Parliament.
These can only be fairly represented and fully brought

before the public and Parliament by Indians themselves, because they only can understand where the shoe pinches, and where certain Acts which are trying to them require to be modified. And the necessity becomes greater, because many a large portion of the administration in India is based upon two or three Acts of Parliament, and as long as Parliament itself does not modify those Acts and does not pay greater attention to the affairs of India than it does at present, there is no chance of the improvement which is so desirable as much for England as for India. Those Acts can be modified in Parliament alone, and it is only on the floor of the House of Commons that they can be fairly discussed, face to face between Englishmen and Indians. The necessity is a very urgent one. Every day that passes makes those evils greater in their effect, and they must be modified as early as possible. Much has been said, on this occasion and outside also, of the great expectations that are formed of me; that I shall do justice to my constituency, and that I shall do my duty to my country. Very kindly you have testified as to what you suppose to be the certainty of my being able to do that. For my own part, I cannot on this occasion say anything about myself, because I enter upon a new career, and upon a new duty, and under entirely new circumstances. How far I may be enabled to perform those duties it is not for me to say, because I do not know. This day next year I may be able to stand before my constituents and give them an account of my stewardship, and I may be able to stand before you, and you will be able then to say whether or not I have fulfilled the expectations which you had formed about me. For the present I can only thank you most sincerely, and take a share in your joy. I assure you that I feel the responsibility, and I only hope that with your indulgence and forbearance I may be able to fulfil some little portion at least of the expectations that have been formed of me. (Loud cheers.) I again thank you most sincerely for the very cordial and kind manner in which you have received this toast.

Mr. T. M. Nair :—

Mr. Chairman, Ladies, and Gentlemen,—The task of proposing the toast of " India and the Indians," has fallen to me this evening. Speaking of India, I cannot revert to the subject without experiencing mingled feelings of pride and sorrow. Everyone who understands anything at all about India's history ought to know that India once was the glory of the world, and is now the pity of it. We cannot help recalling to ourselves how at a time when all Europe was shrouded in darkness, India was the source of life and light to all the nations of the world. (Cheers.) Our forefathers cultivated a system of philosophy which will compare favourably with even the very best system of modern philosophy. And we have evidence in our ancient books to prove that even in those early days our forefathers had devised, and successfully carried out, some forms of consultative if not of representative Government which the British public are not unwilling to grant us at this moment. (Cheers.) But, gentlemen, like Greece and Rome, India had to suffer for her greatness. After the period of India's greatness came the period of India's fall, and " what a fall was there, my countrymen !" But it will be more consonant with our feelings to draw a veil over all those periods in the history of India in which there is nothing but foreign invasions and wars to chronicle. Now, gentlemen, we may thank ourselves that, after all these periods of wars and turmoil, we have placed ourselves under the fostering care of a generous nation We have received no doubt, many advantages from the British Government in India. Mr. Naoroji has touched upon some of them already, and I need not detail them to you. We appreciate them, and we are sincerely thankful for them. But, unfortunately, a foreign rule, even if it should happen to be the very best that could be, is not an unmixed blessing. The people of India have found it to their cost, and it is a problem with our people in India at the present moment as to how to remedy the defects that exist in this foreign administration by a strictly constitutional agitation. To a great extent the problem has been solved. The Indian National Congress, which has existed for the last eight years, has shown the British public and the Parliament what it is to be reasonable. But while it is the fact that the Indian National Congress has done a great deal in the way of advocating beneficial reforms for India and educating the masses of the people, we must admit that certain gentlemen connected with the National Congress have been very ably working in this country also. I refer to the British Committee. It is a significant fact, a fact that we ought to be proud of, that whether we look among the leaders or the Congress party in India or among the committee working in Great Britain, we find one name that is conspicuous, that is the name of Mr. Dadabhai Naoroji, whom we have met to honour this evening. (Cheers.) I need not, gentlemen, detail to you all that Mr. Naoroji has done for India; the Chairman has already done so at some length. But, gentlemen, even at this moment, when we are met here to celebrate Mr. Naoroji's return as representative for Central Finsbury, we ought not to forget the fact that he is only returned for a time, and that the term of his representation will expire. Let us not conceal from ourselves the fact that we shall have to work hard to get him in again. We may have dinners and addresses and all sorts of things, but there must be a determination on the part of every one of us to do our very best to keep Mr. Naoroji in the position in which his constituents of Central Finsbury have placed him. (Cheers.) We may do several things to attain our object, but there is one thing more than another which we should do, that is every Indian living in London should transfer himself to Central Finsbury before the 31st of July. (Cheers and laughter.) I find that the statement is received with some laughter, but it is no laughing matter at all. We ought to see to it that as many Indians as are available should be in Central Finsbury before next year, so as to be placed on the register. We have an example of the same kind of action in Liverpool, where the Irish all cluster in one constituency, and are now able to return a member of their own. I do not mean to say that we are numerically so strong as they are, but we ought to be able to make this position a safe one for Mr. Naoroji. I beg to commend the toast to your acceptance, and trust that you will receive it in an appropriate manner. (Loud cheers.)

Mr. A. A. Hussanally :—

Gentlemen,—To me has been assigned the task of responding to the toast proposed in such eloquent language by my friend, Mr. Nair. I need hardly say that I have the greatest pleasure in doing so, although I wish it had fallen into worthier hands. It is no common event to find Hindus, Mahomedans, Parsis, and Christians, all alike feeling that in the honour conferred upon Mr. Naoroji they have been honoured, and that his success is a matter for the congratulation of them all. Such a feeling, gentlemen, is a most remarkable feature of the progress India has made in recent times. It shows that there is a national feeling growing up up amongst the different communities inhabiting that great peninsula of India. It is true that we have but begun the work of Nationalism; and it is also true that we are making slow but steady advances towards the attainment of that glorious object. India is, gentlemen, at present in a state of transition; she is no longer the India of the East, nor has she yet become the India of the West. But Western culture and Western civilisation are gradually changing the aspect of the whole country. It would, no doubt, be interesting to inquire into the causes that have operated to bring about this change. And such an inquiry is all the more interesting when it results in the conviction that we owe this growth of national feeling and national prosperity to the advent of British rule in India. The different races of India are taking more kindly to each other because they are living under one Government, and that the most enlightened and humane Government that has ever ruled an alien race because they have now easy means of intercommunication by railways, post, and telegraph, which have destroyed the local feeling of isolation, and, above all, because they have a Free Press, which has been a powerful factor in the progress of India. But the greatest of all blessings which we have enjoyed under British rule, and one which deserves to be mentioned separately, is the Western education which we have received and are receiving, and which will enable us to work out our own destiny in the future. But for this education we should have been nowhere. And to this education mainly we owe the general progress which we have hitherto made. In this direction, however, gentlemen, we have yet to do a great deal. Education is spreading in India, but it has not yet made such strides as we should like it to do. No soil is better fitted to receive Western education than India. Possessing as we do the sources of the two great classical languages of the East, we are in a peculiarly advantageous position to enrich our own languages by modern ideas, which we imbibe from Western learning. With this object in view, I think we should encourage as much as possible the translation of European works into Indian languages, so that the Western ideas might reach the masses directly, and open to them a new world of thought, culture and science.

Wherever the education imparted has been a broad and liberal education, the results have been most satisfactory. But education has still vast conquests to make. We have yet to break the social barriers of caste, we have yet to override superstition and conquer prejudices, and above all we have yet to elevate the social position of the women of India. Here lies a vast field for us who are all inspired with a sense of their duty to their country, and are anxious to work for her welfare. For I firmly believe that no political reform in India is likely to confer a real benefit upon the people until social reform goes side by side, and no social reform is possible until the lot of Indian women is improved and their moral and social condition raised. The speaker concluded with a quotation from Professor Max Mülier's writings.

Mr. Martin Wood :—

I only wish to say one word on this occasion. I should not like it to pass over without giving my testimony on behalf of India and the Indians to your representative this evening. Of all Europeans present I have, perhaps, known Mr. Dadabhai Naoroji more years than any one. I have known him under many different circumstances, some of which have been so eloquently described by our chairman. In regard to this toast I wish, as a European, to join with you in responding to it, and in cherishing the spirit of true patriotism which will raise the Indians in their political discussions above those objections and criticisms that have often been brought against them. There can be no more elevating thought than that of this community of the natives of India for the promotion of public objects. Mr. Naoroji is himself an illustration, and a striking one, of the diversities that exist in that country, and we see how thoroughly he unites all the chief qualities of the Indian races. (Cheers.)

Mr. A. Ghosh :—

Mr. Chairman, Ladies and Gentlemen,—At this late hour of the evening I will not detain you long. The toast I have to propose is an important one : it is the toast of the ladies. (Loud cheers.) I observe by the enthusiastic manner in which you have received the announcement of the toast that it certainly appeals to your heartfelt sympathies. Ladies are an important part of the constitution of Indian society ; they have always been so,

and they have always been held in the highest esteem and
respect from the most ancient times. We have in the
history of ancient India examples of distinguished women ;
we have examples of women who have distinguished themselves in philosophy, in mathematics, and in letters. It
is a common belief in Europe that the women in India are
not treated with that respect by which alone the true civilisation and advancement of a country can be estimated.
Whatever be the effect of some social customs in India at
the present day, I am sure no man who is conversant with
the origin of those customs will deny for a single moment
that they are due to a desire to protect, to guard and to
foster women rather than to repress and keep them down.
(Cheers.) In Hindoo society woman is respected as much
as in the society of the most civilised community of the
world. (Cheers.) That woman bears a high character in
India, whether as mother, as wife, or as sister, there can be
no doubt. I only make this remark because we very often
hear attacks made in English reviews on the treatment of
Indian women. But in this matter I do not wish to refer
you to any authority, except the authority of women
themselves. If there be anything in Indian customs which
need reform, that reform certainly must come from within,
and it must be spontaneous. If our women are to be advanced, if they are to take a prominent part in political
and social movements in India, the most important thing
is that they should receive higher education. I believe
there is a great future for women, and I have no doubt you
will agree with me when I say that our women will be
the making of India. The great Napoleon on a memorable
occasion once declared that what France wanted was good
mothers, and I think you will agree with me when I say
that what India wants is good mothers. I am far from
saying that Indian mothers are not good, but what I mean
is this, that we must train up a race of highly intellectual
and enlightened mothers if we desire the regeneration of
India. I will not detain you longer, but I desire to thank
you sincerely for the manner in which you have received
this toast. (Cheers.)

Mr. J. N. Roy :—

Mr. Chairman, in rising to respond to the toast proposed
by my friend, Mr. Ghosh, I have but a few words to say.
If we were not too much fenced by etiquette, I have no

doubt, nay, I am sure that one of the ladies present would have willingly and gladly responded to what Mr. Ghosh has said. But I suppose we must not break through any custom, although there would be greater honour in its breach than in its observance; I have therefore great pleasure in responding to the toast. Personally, I feel flattered in being the spokesman of the ladies, and I feel sûre that I interpret their feelings correctly when I say that they appreciate this toast deeply. They recognise in it our willingness, the willingness of educated Indians to let them take part in the social, educational, and political reform of our country. If we were not in England, where our numbers are small, I have no doubt that instead of having nine or ten ladies present, we should have had as many hundreds, uniting with us to celebrate this interesting occasion. Every day Indian women are learning to trust themselves more and more, and are becoming more and more willing to work with us, and at the same time to work out their own destiny. They recognise the great fact that the fate of India lies as much with them as with the men of the country. They know that the cradle is under their influence, and they have found out that this is an influence which determines a good or a bad citizen. Yes, they are willing to work for us and with us, and they are sensible of the welcome that is accorded to them. I thank you on behalf of the ladies, and at the same time congratulate myself on being their spokesman. (Cheers.)

Rai Tej Narayan Singh Bahadur proposed the health of the Chairman, who briefly responded, and the company then separated.

3. Mr. Gladstone on Mr. Naoroji.

Speaking at West Calder respecting the loss of some Liberal seats by Liberal disunion, Mr. Gladstone said :— "Lord Salisbury one day spoke in contempt of black men. It is a curious fact that what Lord Salisbury called a black man has just been returned, to my great satisfaction, for a division of London, and now, if some of us think that black men politically are not advanced up to your limit, very likely it is true because they have not had the practice. (Here Mr. Gladstone's audience laughed, though why goodness only knows.) But I will tell you what, if all the black men in the world were set to elect representatives of Parliament, they could not execute or

devise a proceeding more worthy of the disapproval of
every rational man than what has been enacted in Perth
and Glasgow and in Salford.

VII.

Mr. Naoroji's Maiden Speech in Parliament.

Mr. Dadabhai Naoroji's first speech in the Commons
seems to have been spoken with the ease of an Englishman
and the fervour of an Oriental. The following is the text
of his maiden speech :—

"Mr. Naoroji said it might be thought rather rash and
unwise on his part to stand up in this House so soon after
his admission, but his excuse was that he was under a certain necessity to do so. A very great and unique event
had happened in connection with India. For the first time
in the history of British rule in India, an Indian was admitted into this House as a member for an English constituency. (Cheers.) The spirit of British rule, the instinct
of British justice and generosity, when Britain first took
the matter of Indian government seriously in hand about
the beginning of this century, deliberately decided that
India should be governed on the lines of British freedom
and justice. Steps were taken without any hesitation to
introduce Western education, civilization, and political
institutions into that country. The result was that aided
by a noble language, the youth of India began to be educated, a great movement of political thought set in, and a
new life was infused into the country which had been
decaying for centuries. They had given to India freedom
of speech and enabled Indians to stand before their British
rulers and to represent their case in clear and open language whenever they felt aggrieved in any matter, and the
ultimate result, so to speak, was that an Indian stood
before them in this House, a member of the Parliament of
the British Empire able to state his views openly and
freely. The glory and credit of this great event, which had
thrilled India from one end to the other, the new life, the
joy, and ecstasy of India at the present moment—all was
theirs. He stood there in the name of India to thank
British rulers that they had made it possible for an Indian
to stand before this House with the conviction—though
he had no numbers of votes behind him to influence its

action—that whenever he had any grievance to bring forward supported by just and proper reasons he would always find a large number of other members ready to support him and to concede the justice that he asked. (Cheers.) The name of Central Finsbury would never be forgotten by India. The event of his election had strengthened the loyalty and attachment of India ten times more than if 100,000 European soldiers had been sent to protect that country. (Cheers.) The moral force of which the right honorable Member for Mid Lothian spoke was the golden thread by which India was held by the British Power; as long as India was satisfied with the justice and honour of Britain, so long would the Indian Empire endure. He hoped the connection between England and India, which formed in fact five-sixths of the British Empire, might continue long and with benefit to both countries. (Cheers.)"

VIII.
Opinions of the Press.

1. Indian.

The following notes to the *Indian Spectator* will be read with interest :—

By the time this reaches you, the statistical map of the entire electoral campaign will be spread before you, so that you will know better than I can predict. As matters stand at present, the Salisbury-Balfour majority is reduced from 68 to 28 ; and, if Liberal prophets are correct, that may yet be reduced to a minority of about twenty. If so, the result will be indecisive ; there will be a short sharp episode of parliamentary confusion, and within a few months the whole struggle will have to be gone through again. Meantime, your people will care nothing about the pans and kettles of our party potsherds, compared with the great fact that your G. O. M. is saved, "as if by fire." You must bless those three true Imperialist voters of Central Finsbury who secured this result, or rather the eight whose votes reversed Captain Penton's position. The numbers are much higher in both cases—last time 2,245 and 2,240, respectively : this time D. 2,959 and P. 2,956. When we consider Captain Penton's inevitable influence as ground landlord in a large portion of the district, that he was in possession, that he is personally popular, and that he had carriages galore sent by the Marquis of Salisbury, and a Duke or two, and other shining lights of the aristocracy, this hard-fought political victory is sufficiently striking. Amongst the names of those carriage senders is one that might well have been absent, that of the Rev. Algernon Bourke, brother of your still honoured Viceroy, who might for decency's sake have sent his vehicle elsewhere. But that is a trifle. The substantial advantage that came at the eleventh hour was conversion of the little band of local obstructors, who, it must be cheerfully acknowledged, did their part at last like true Britons and came to the forefront of the fight. It was a great pleasure to me to hear the excellent speech of their leader, Mr. Walton, last Saturday night, on behalf of your representative, and again on Tuesday night, at the final demonstration, when, as Chairman, he made a most effective appeal to the same effect. It was good to see, also, the late intractable candidate, Mr. F. Ford, come forward and gracefully support his more popular rival. Perhaps, we may thank his talented wife for that, who bears her own name honoured amongst women journalists. Your citizen, Mr. M. M. Bhownagri, also made a good speech on this occasion in support of the candidate.

Speaking of women, it may be most suitable, in the brief space that I can occupy with details, to give some notice of the four lady orators who contributed so much to the triumphant success of that final meeting on Tuesday night. First, there was Miss Colenso, who, though she does not find the platform congenial, speaks in a quiet lady-like manner, and made a very genial impression. She spoke of Mr. Dadabhai as a representative of the remote, the weak and the unrepresented millions of the Empire and as a fitting supporter of the venerable Liberal leader. She alluded to her own sympathy as a Natal Colonist with the principle of Home Rule as the only true means of binding the Empire together, and warmly commended her own loyal but grievously ill-used Zulus with touching references to her revered father. Very different in matter and manner was Mrs. Bradlaugh-Bonner, who spoke with dignified filial affection of your last champion and of his deep, almost overwhelming, devotion to the Indian people of which she had such intimate knowledge. It was thus as a pioneer of more effective and reforming administration of India that

Charles Bradlaugh, though dead, yet spoke by the mouth
of his devoted daughter. Nothing could have been more
fitting than her noble bearing and well-chosen remarks.
The other two lady speakers were of very different types,
illustrating the qualities of the divers races that this great
Empire has gathered under its wide wings and sheltering
arm. Words would fail to describe the skill, "the go"
and the vivacity of the young Irish Countess Emily Keary,
as with mingled humour and enthusiasm she pleaded the
cause of social reform amongst the masses of the people,
and, with enhanced eloquence, the cause of her own emerald
isle. The next is no stranger to Finsbury ; as soon as the
Chairman mentioned that they should have an address from
the lady who had thrilled them all the other night, the whole
meeting from floor to the topmost gallery cheered with might
and main, renewed again as the lady orator stepped forward and gracefully responded to the plaudits. This is Mrs.
Wynford Philipps (née Nora Gerstenberg), wife of the rising
member for Lanarkshire. She is proud of her ancient daring
race—it would be vain to doubt for a moment, her Hebrew
origin which is revealed in every feature, in every
movement, and gives even an oriental effect to her fashion-
able costume, but, above all, in her intellectual forcing and
moving eloquence. To those of us who have had to grope
our way step by step through the complicated social
problems of the day, like a revelation to hear her illuminate
them in flowing it was language, skilful, though only
implied, argument interspersed with flashing sentences of
eloquence, whilst the meeting swayed to and fro with an
enthusiasm that surprises one amidst the ordinary dingy
life of Finsbury. There is in her gestures and manner
when roused, as on this occasion, that which reminds one
even of "the divine Sarah" and the traditions of the un-
equalled tragedienne Rachel. There was one passage in
which she touched on the theme of religious equality—" the
right of every one to follow the light given to lead through
life to God"—which might be said to reach the sublime,
as in the rising sentences of the full deep voice, with
accumulating gesture she raised her hands above her head
as if in appeal to Heaven itself. There was indicated the
native genius of the true dramatist ; and if the opulent
condition of herself and her husband did not forbid, one
might predict her inevitable appearance as a successor of
the still enthralling Bernhardt. When Mrs. Phillips

finally withdrew from front of the platform, the whole audience rose in such furore of enthusiasm as one has only witnessed after a peroration of John Bright's and one or two other orators of our period.

You may well query what had this demonstration to do with the modest business-like programme of your plain-spoken representative. But Mrs. Phillips did not forget that, and it chimed in with the social and industrial aspirations of the proletariat which he is bound to support in his own reasonable fashion. He made a brief speech on this occasion suitable to the purpose, and other speakers of the masculine order gave appropriate addresses, including one from a young Irish doctor which was racy of the verdant island. There was also a Church *padre* who gave an impressive short speech; and one of your former (European) citizens gave his testimony to the qualities of your representative and to the confidence that all India reposes in him. Since his election has been announced, it is quite reassuring to notice how the event has elicited the approval of the press, not omitting some Conservative journals. It may now be hoped that Mr. Dadabhai will go to sleep for a fortnight, as he stands in the utmost need of rest after his protracted efforts of weeks and months. It was gratifying to see that the Committee had active assistance from many Indians now in town who worked hard in the arduous secretariat and organising business that had to be gone through. You know about all this better than most of us.

The British Parliament is the custodian of the Englishman's concerns, religious, social and political. It has the right to legislate on these matters. A member of Parliament goes into it to represent the religions, political and social interests of his constituency. The electors of Central Finsbury have entrusted all these interests of theirs to a *foreigner*, alien in race and creed, and one of a subject people in addition. And yet in this country some of our patriots, passing for good Hindoos, would avail themselves of a foreigner for political ends only, but turn their backs on him, treat him as a *Mlecha* when the other ends are under discussion! Mr. Dadabhai's election surely teaches us several lessons, not the least important of which is this, that we should do what the electors of Central Finsbury have done—that we should, so far from being ashamed of foreign guidance in all matters, be they religious, social or political, welcome light and help whencesoever they come.

One other lesson, again, of the election should not be lost sight of. A great deal was rightly made at the Town Hall meeting of the fact that several English ladies—notably, Miss Florence Nightingale, "the heroine of the 19th century," Miss Evans Bell, and Mrs. Josephine Butler —did their best to secure Mr. Dadabhai's election. We are all grateful to these noble-hearted, generous-spirited ladies; and when we are praising them, thanking them and blessing them for their generous help, let us not forget that it is their cultured intelligence which has enabled them to help the foreigner. After this, will some of our reactionary patriots continue to talk of the evils of female education and enlightenment, and the blessings of the Zenana system, female ignorance and degradation.— *Suboda Patrika.*

The return of Mr. Dadabhai Naoroji to the House of Commons as the representative of Central Finsbury is one of the most striking events that have occurred in connexion with the recent General Election. As his majority was a very narrow one, a scrutiny of the votes was demanded, and it was possible that Mr. Naoroji would not after all sit in the new Parliament; still, even if the result of the scrutiny had been unfavourable, it is a striking thing that half of the electors of an English constituency should have voted for a native of India as their parliamentary representative. Mr. Naoroji has now been revenged upon Lord Salisbury, whose tasteless and absurd remark of some years ago has doubtless assisted him not a little in his candidature. His election is a testimony to the growing cosmopolitanism of Great Britain, and it may well be that it will help some to realise that India forms an integral part of a great Empire. In India it has evoked great enthusiasm and has occasioned much rejoicing, especially among those who may be termed advanced politicians. This is not unnatural, but it should afford food for serious thought to some of those that the first Indian to enter Parliament is not a Hindu but a Parsee. During the recent agitation in connexion with marriage questions, it was carefully pointed out, especially in Bengal, that Mr. Malabari, who took such a prominent part in that agitation, was as a Parsee, an alien in race and religion. This was of course true, but it will doubtless now be found convenient to forget the fact, and it will be indeed surprising if we are not now favoured with the argument that because Mr. Naoroji is fit to represent an English constituency, India is already fit for representative institutions.—*The Christian College Magazine.*

All honour to Central Finsbury for returning Mr. Dadabhai Naoroji to Parliament. It is no importance whether the majority is three or three thousand for the triumph : the principle is what we look to. It is for this that Mr. Dadabhai Naoroji at considerable personal sacrifice has been fighting for the last seven years, and this success is a source of congratulation, not only to himself personally and his friends and immediate supporters, but also to the whole country. The 'Black Man's audacity' in seeking entrance into St. Stephen's' no longer astounds the British elector, and the generous action of Central Finsbury opens out a new era in the modern political history of India—an era the importance of which it is impossible to over-estimate, and the result of which may be much more far-reaching than we or our successors in the immediate future can imagine.—*Hindu Patriot.*

Had it not been for the quarrel with Mr. Schnadhorst, the majority would have been larger ; and hence the small majority is the more significant, for it proves that notwithstanding all election dodges and external obstacles, the cause of truth and justice is sure to win the hearts of the British people. The electors of Central Finsbury, by choosing a native of India as their representative, have clearly testified to the world that they could rise above petty considerations of race or nationality, where interests of 288 millions of their fellowmen were at stake. They have thus not only laid India under deep obligations, but have also immortalized themselves for all times to come. The election of a native of a dependency like India to the British Parliament is an event, unique in the history, not only of England or India, but of the whole world. It marks a new stage in the struggles of India to regain political privileges; and hence the 6th July of 1892 will always remain a red-lettered day in the annals of the British Empire.—*Mahratta.*

We are very glad that Mr. Dadabhai Naoroji has been elected, but we should see that the incident does not turn our heads. There is no doubt of it that he is the fittest man in India to represent her people. It is quite possible that there are people who might have preferred other Indian gentlemen having other qualifications and advantages, but Mr. Dadabhai Naoroji has had training that many have not. It gives us great comfort to reflect that a very good Indian has been selected, and that he is not the man to bring shame or humiliation upon his country.—*Amrita Bazaar Patrika.*

The most cheerful piece of news to which we had all been looking forward with the most anxious expectations for some years past—and most especially since the dissolution of the last Parliament—has at length been flashed out to us, and it has by this time spread like electrical currents throughout the nooks and corners of India that Mr. Dadabhai Naoroji, that fearless and disinterested champion of our political rights and privileges, has been elected for Central Finsbury by a majority of three votes. In the personal career of the Grand Old Man of India,—Mr. Dadabhai's return to Parliament is the crowning edifice of his just and laudable ambition; and we congratulate him from the bottom of our hearts on this rare honour done to him in behalf of the two hundred and fifty-four millions of Her Majesty's loyal but voiceless subjects of British India. It is a merited recompense of a long and laborious life of an eminently exalted stamp, spent in the people's cause at the most inconceivable sacrifice of personal comfort and convenience.—*Gujarat Mitra.*

All India will hail with delight the election of Mr. Dadabhai Naoroji as member for Central Finsbury. The delight on this side of India will be more, because he is a citizen of Bombay, among the Parsees still greater because the very first Indian to enter Parliament is a member of their own race. . . He bore Mr. Schnadhorst's conduct with heroic patience and fortitude, and with his energy

14

unabated at the age of sixty-seven he continued to pursue his object, trying his persuasive powers even among Conservative dames, and not altogether without success as we are informed by a friend—to secure the abstention of their husbands from the poll, if, indeed, they could not give him their active support. " Wooed and won !" Let this be his motto henceforth. It signalizes the crowning act of his life which will also be the most memorable. And he has done a signal service to the Liberal party in spite of the cold indifference of its leader. He has wrested a victory for them in a borough within the metropolitan area.—*Rast Goftar.*

Whatever may be our feelings with regard to the conduct of the Liberal party in the matter of our countryman's candidature towards the Liberal electors of Central Finsbury, we can have only one feeling, the feeling of the deepest, most heartfelt, gratitude. It was they who cheered him on in his uphill contest. It was they who stood by him in the supreme moment of crisis. It was they who endorsed the claims of a poor Indian as against those of one of their own countrymen. And, finally, it was they who made Mr. Dadabhai Naoroji's success. We can never be sufficiently grateful to the Liberal electors of Central Finsbury. In the late Mr. Bradlaugh, the constituency of Northampton possessed an English Member for India. But in Mr. Dadabhai Naoroji, Central Finsbury may take a reasonable pride in having a regular Indian Member for India.—*Indian Mirror.*

The return of Mr. Dadabhai Naoroji to Parliament by the electors of Central Finsbury is an event which will excite the profoundest interest throughout India. That a native of this country, one of the so-called conquered population, should be elected by the free will of a number of Englishmen to fill a seat in their national legislature, the most ancient and august representative assembly in the world, which controls not the affairs of India but those of the Imperial country itself, its colonies and dependencies and the numerous and weighty affairs of that world-wide Empire, is an occurrence over which the Indian people might well congratulate themselves. Verily it does look

romantic, that the old Parsee gentleman of Bombay, after
his sixtieth year, should woo an English constituency to
represent it in the Imperial legislature, and that, moved
by the wooer's persistency, courage and ability, the constituency itself should be generous and catholic enough to
prefer that fireworshipping Indian fellow-subject of theirs
to a countryman of their own, to one of themselves,
speaking their language and following their religion, and
that the Parsee member should debate and vote equally
with Mr. Gladstone and Lord Salisbury, really reads like
an incident in a romance, and is a singular monument of
the splendid elasticity of the British constitution, of the
generous instincts of the Englishmen, and of the liberal
sentiments, unparalleled in the history of any other Imperial
nation, which animate Britain's rule of this country. Such
a thing is possible only in England. We do not indeed
exaggerate the practical benefit of Mr. Dadabhai speaking
and voting as one out of six hundred and odd members of
the House of Commons. But there can be no doubt of the
importance of the precedent thus established by the generous
action of the Finsbury Liberals. If one Indian can be
returned as a member, why cannot half-a-dozen be so returned and thus India given, in that great assembly, a
substantial if not quite adequate voice. We are confident
that Mr. Dadabhai will be a source of much wholesome
influence on those that speak on Indian topics in the
House. No man living knows more of the administrative
principles and details of this country; and with the extraordinary power with which Mr. Dadabhai can speak
and debate, he will inspire a wholesome fear, and will be
looked to as an authoritative exponent of Indian feeling
and as one whose opinions are entitled to higher weight
than the opinions of any other members can command.
Now only does England complete her claim to be called
an Imperial country. The tie that binds India to her
ruling country is no longer the mere sentiment of loyalty,
ever so genuine and profound, but is the real constitutional
equality attested by the actual presence of an Indian
member in the Imperial Council. Nor can either England
or India find a better representative of the people of this
country than Mr. Dadabhai. No Indian surpasses him in
culture, knowledge, courage or sobriety of judgment; and
his character both as a private man and as a citizen is so
high and so spotless that the feeling he inspires in his

countrymen is one almost verging on adoration. The
honourable and learned gentlemen representing England,
Wales, Scotland, Ireland, amidst whom the solitary
Bombay Parsee will sit and participate in the proceedings,
will find in their interesting colleague a very worthy fellow-
subject who will bring credit to the constituency that
elected him, to the Parliament that bears with him, and to
the millions of his fellow-countrymen whose aspirations He
shares and whose capacity and loyalty he represents. May
the generous and just rule of Britain over India last as
long as the sun and moon to accomplish her great mission
in this country and add endlessly to her name and glory.
—*The Hindu.*

The indirect results of the election of Mr. Dadabhai
promise to be of more moment than the direct ones. It is
not only the *people* of India that rejoice at his success, but
the *Princes* of India also seem to join heartily in the
congratulations that are offered to our Grand Old Man.
The Indian noblemen form the most exclusive and in some
respects the most backward aristocracy, and if they are
educated in the force and power of democracy, the good
that will accrue to India would be indeed immense. The
Princes of India, wealthy and honoured as they are, now
see how without those adventitious and accidental advantages they inherited from their forefathers, true public
spirit and enlightenment can win for itself a place which
they may well envy and which it is not probably in their
power to aspire to attain. The educative influence of Mr.
Dadabhai's election seems to us to deserve special mention.
Fortunately as a set off against Lord Salisbury and the friends
of Captain Penton, the Maharajah Gaekwar was in London.
While Mr. Dadabhai's opponent had the countenance of
Lord Salisbury, the Gaekwar did what he could and placed
his carriages at the disposal of his countryman. The
spirit of patriotism thus evoked is worthy of appreciation.
And the London Correspondent of the *Bombay Gazette*
writes :—" Among those who sent telegrams are the
Gaekwar of Baroda, who I see it stated lent Mr. Dadabhai
carriages on the polling day, the Nawab Sahib of Junaghad,
the Thakore Sahib of Gondal, and the Dewan of Baroda.
Since then Sir Asman Jah, Prime Minister of Hyderabad,
has cabled :—" Accept my cordial congratulations." The
Nawab Fatch Nawaz Jung, the Home Secretary of the

same State, had previously sent a similar message. Thus have the Indian Princes shared the joy of the humblest citizens of Madras. Whoever thought four years ago that Sir Asman Jah and Mr. Dadabhai would exchange courtesies! Truly the significance of Mr. Dadabhai's success is beyond the ken of ordinary vision. To the Englishmen who are a united nation and whose glories are written in undying characters the solitary Parsee that sits under the ægis of Mr. Gladstone may not be more than a two days' wonder. But to us who are aware of the disintegrating influences of Indian society, who know but too well what rank disunion and hopeless apathy prevail among our countrymen, every incident which makes for producing a feeling of brotherhood among them, every constitutional move which by the magic of its practical effect brings on a common platform the prince and the peasant, the Mahomedan aristocrat and the Hindu or Parsee plebian, is a God-send and affects us for good. Viewed in this light, the return to Parliament of Mr. Dadabhai is full of instruction and encouragement. The Anglo-Indian cynic who is suffering from the " Congress windbag " on the brain and who regards with alarm the assertive qualities of his Indian fellow-subject may write as he chooses. But this does not injure us. If the poetic instinct of the nation is not dead, and if there are any Sanskrit scholars of high attainments in the country who have the ability of their illustrious forefathers, a sacred literature might yet arise in India having for its subject the Queen's reign and indicating the success achieved—a work which must be fit to take its place side by side with our greatest works of old, so that the wanderer along the streets who stops for a few minutes to hear the Brahmin recite the victories of Rama, may from the same Brahmin story-teller hear the glory of the Parliaments of the West. This is one mode of nationalising foreign ideals.—*The Hindu.*

The success of Mr. Dadabhai Naoroji is certainly an event over which the whole nation may rejoice. We remember what hard words were said of our veteran patriot on the last occasion when he failed in the elections of 1886. The more rabid of Anglo-Indian papers, which are always on the look-out for some incident which will enable them to point the finger of scorn to the Indian, philosophised on

the unpractical idea of a native of India entering the
Parliament. It would seem that if for nothing else, at
least to gag for the moment the mouths of these calumni-
ators of the Indian race, Providence had willed otherwise,
and the good voters of Central Finsbury who won the seat
for Mr. Dadabhai deserve all the honour and respect which
we can show them for the great confidence which they
have reposed in our distinguished and illustrious Parseé
brother. The *Pioneer* received to-day writes in a tone of
bitter but suppressed disappointment. The *London Times*
with all its intense conservatism is a more generous critic
of Indians than the savage *Pi*. The latter affects to doubt
" the wisdom of the 2959 voters who have sent " Mr. Dadha-
bai " to St. Stephens " and finds fault with the *Times* for
the observation it made that the return of a native of
India to Parliament " is interesting and even romantic."
Such an exhibition of needless petulance and narrow mind-
edness is not likely to draw closer the cords that bind the
rulers and the ruled in India. The *Pi* only serves to make
itself ridiculous in the eyes of all fair-minded people,
Europeans or Indians, and to widen the gulf which sepa-
rates the two races in India. But our countrymen can
well afford to ignore the insulting language of blind parti-
sans like the *Pioneer*, and even to forget it in the unmistaka-
ble evidence of English generosity furnished by the citizens of Central Finsbury. It is of the utmost importance
that the whole of India, from Cape Comorin to the Himala-
yas, should be stirred to spontaneous activity and our countrymen in all parts of India should devise national modes
of congratulating themselves, the Liberal voters of Central
Finsbury and Mr. Dadabhai. Telegrams should be sent in
hundreds and thousands to the Liberal Association of Finsbury through Mr. Dadabhai, thanking them for their
appreciation of the merits of our countryman. Public
meetings should be held in all parts of the country, in
towns and villages, where the resolution should be ratified.
All this must be taken in hand without loss of time. Pro-
crastination and delay, which are the immemorial curse of
India, ought to be avoided. There must be such a regular
shower of telegrams in Central Finsbury during the next
few weeks, that they ought to mark an event in themselves
and leave no doubt of the national awakening in India and
the spirit of enlarged nationality that is just budding forth
in the hearts of the Indians. Two distinct duties devolve

upon us. One is to demonstrate our confidence in Mr. Dadabhai and thank the voters of Finsbury. The other is to express in a fitting manner the joy we feel. Various schemes are suggested to achieve the latter end. A proposal is made that the 5th of August, on which date Mr. Dadabhai will take his seat in Parliament, should be observed as a day of national festival this year and in the years to come. It is also thought necessary to present Mr. Dadabhai with a purse to compensate in a manner for the expenses which he has incurred and to strengthen his hands. But to do all these, our countrymen must be roused to enthusiasm, and we shall be glad to have substantial proof of the same. The possibility of a native of India entering the august House of Commons has been effectively demonstrated, and this fact in itself is worthy of the most marked recognition and an exuberance of spirit similar to that which Lord Ripon's departure from India evoked.

2. ENGLISH.

" The appearance of a native of India in the British Parliament is an interesting and almost romantic event, if romance can enter into politics. The experiment will be watched with attention none the less, because it cannot in the nature of things be frequently repeated."—*The Times.*

" Mr. Naoroji is one of a small tribe of Persians, now eighty-nine thousand in number, who live and prosper in Western India, under the British flag, but who have no relation, either in race, creed or social customs, to the Hindus, and are regarded by the Mussulmans with an acute traditional dislike, which has led more than once to serious rioting. We have no objection whatever to Parsees, who are perhaps the most advanced people in Asia, and who are of necessity loyal to the flag which protects them from extermination; but a Parsee is no more a representative of Indians, than a Nestorian Christian would be of Ottomans. Mr. Naoroji, to begin with, professes to be an extreme Radical, and if there is a set of ideas to the world antipathetic to the Hindu or Mussulman, it is that described as English Radicalism."—*The Spectator.*

"This gentleman, Mr. Naoroji, is a little harmless-looking person. His complexion is swarthy, though its hue is naturally deepened by the setting of white or silvery hair, which invests Mr. Naoroji with an expression of benevolence. His manners are in keeping with his appearance, and there is a limpid softness in his speech."—*The Western Daily Press of Bristol.*

———————

"What is them"?
"Parsees; they worship the sun."
"Do they? Then they must have a precious easy time of it over here"!

"Such, we believe, is the substance of a skit that appeared in *Punch* some years ago. The election of Mr. Naoroji to Westminster recalled it to our mind, for we cannot help thinking that, whatever spare moments the hon. member may hitherto have enjoyed, he will find plenty to do to occupy his leisure as soon as he takes his seat in Parliament. It is certainly an odd choice for an English constituency to make. Is Mr. Naoroji supposed to represent our Eastern Empire or Finsbury—millions or thousands only? Will he pose as the thin end of the wedge of Imperial Federation, or is he the first link forged of a chain of Home Rule for India? Events are hurried on so now-a-days that if Mr. Gladstone's policy is carried to its logical conclusion, we may wake up one fine morning to find that English members are in a minority in the Imperial Parliament, and that we are legislated for by our former dependencies. We shall be curious to read what the Vernacular Press of India have to say on the subject."—*The Bristol Times.*

———————

"The elections of Wednesday have contributed some new members of distinction to the House of Commons. First and foremost is Lord Salisbury's 'black man,' Mr. Naoroji. His return is a personal rebuke to the Premier for a personal insult and a sneer at our fellow Indian subjects. Mr. Naoroji is a Parsee merchant of high character and education, and his skin, as a matter of fact, is as white as Lord Salisbury's. He is the first Indian that has been elected to the House of Commons, and his choice will give immense satisfaction throughout our Indian empire."—*The Bradford Observer.*

"The most interesting London victory of Wednesday was that which made Mr. Naoroji—the Parsee gentleman who became famous because of his association with Lord Salisbury's cruel and vulgar remarks about 'black men' —a member of the British Legislature. It is true that the majority to which he has been returned for Central Finsbury is a very small one, but a majority larger only by two votes kept a Tory in for the seat during six eventful years, and it is not likely that the small margin of votes by which it has been wrested from the Tories will in any way cripple Mr. Naoroji's usefulness in the Imperial Parliament. The news of his success was received with great enthusiasm. For a time the issue was doubtful, and it would have done Lord Salisbury good to have heard the loud and repeated cheers which were given for his black man by the Flint Street crowds while the correct return was being anxiously awaited. When the matter was at length placed beyond doubt, a roar went up from thousands of throats: and it would almost seem from the half-benignant, half-scornfully patronising tone in which the *Times* hails his appearance as a British legislator as if the echoes of the demonstration had penetrated Printing House Square. At any rate the *Times* deigns to remark that 'the appearance of a native of India in the British Parliament is an interesting and almost romantic event, if romance can enter into politics. The experiment will be watched with attention none the less, because it cannot, in the nature of things, be frequently repeated.' This is remarkably polite, considering the quarter from which it comes; but the fact of the matter is the Unionist press is dropping some of the bluster with which it started the fight. The *Times* was very nasty at the beginning. There are signs that it will be very humble before the end."— *Leeds Mercury.*

"The return of Mr. Dadabhai Naoroji for Central Finsbury has much significance. For one thing, it is another of those Liberal gains in the Metropolis which are steadily showing that London is waking up to the claims of justice and truth; but most people will regard it as a special slap in the face for Lord Salisbury. One of that statesman's most blazing indiscretions was his contemptuous reference to this esteemable gentleman as 'black man.' The electors of Central Finsbury have clearly proved to Mr. Naoroji's countrymen that they, at least, are free from the stupid and illiberal prejudice of colour, and that they have also shown their appreciation of the Prime Minister's delicate wit by giving him its subject as a fellow-legislator, which must be a galling thought to the Marquis."—*Scottish Leader.*

" In our files by this week's Australian Mail we notice in the letter of a London gossip a political prophecy that looks curious now in the light of the actual fact. The writer, referring to Mr. Labouchere's efforts to restore peace and unity in the Liberal ranks of Central Finsbury, says :—' Labby calmly advises Mr. Naoroji to get out, but the coloured gentleman wont do this, because although he does not expect to poll more than 300 votes altogether, Mr. Naoroji runs an Anglo-Indian newspaper in London, and obtained support for his journal from India on the strength of his being the accepted Liberal candidate for Finsbury.' Alas ! for the prophet of two months ago, Mr. Naoroji polled ten times three hundred votes, and is, to-day, a member for Finsbury."—*The Sunday Sun.*

" Mr. Naoroji's election for Finsbury is not quite so ridiculous as if that unenlightened constituency had sent a Bengali Baboo into Parliament. That is the best that can be said for it.

*   *   *   *

" Meanwhile Central Finsbury should be ashamed of itself at having publicly confessed that there was not in the whole of the division an Englishman, a Scotchman, a Welshman or an Irishman as worthy of their votes as this Fire-Worshipper from Bombay."—*St. Stephen's Review.*

" The manner in which Mr. Naoroji's election to the Imperial Parliament has been received in India has a significance and importance far outweighing his personal qualities, admirable as they undoubtedly are. It shows conclusively that the educated people of India look to the Parliament of Great Britain and Ireland with confidence for the redress of their grievances. It dispels the sinister suggestions of disloyalty so recklessly associated with the movement in India, the object of which is to enable competent natives to exercise the privileges of sharing in the government of their own country. . . . . . If the Congress party contemplated any action not strictly legal and constitutional, they would be indifferent to the composition of the House of Commons. The fact that they have been excited to an unusual pitch of enthusiasm by seeing one of their number returned to it demonstrates their faith in the integrity of the empire and the sense of justice of the British people."— *The Daily Chronicle.*

"They (the Indians) have one of their own kindred— an able patriot held in high esteem by his countrymen— who will watch their interests and help the Liberals to carry reforms for the benefit of India. The delight with which Mr. Naoroji's return has been received by the Congress party in India is a proof of the confidence they have in the British Parliament to redress their wrongs in a constitutional way. Besides especially guarding India's interests, Mr. Naoroji, as a very good Radical, will be a loyal supporter of the Liberals."—*The Star.*

"The election (of Mr. Naoroji) is at once remarkable and acceptable. To Lord Salisbury, indeed, the return of his ' black man ' will, we suppose, be somewhat of a mortification. For it was of Mr. Naoroji that the Prime Minister doubted ' if we have yet got to that point where a British constituency will elect a black man to represent them,' and said that ' at all events he was a man of another race, who was very unlikely to represent an English community.' But though of another race, he is of the same allegiance ; and the return to the Imperial Parliament of a native of India, as informal representative of the millions of Her Majesty's subjects in that empire, even if it should not mark an epoch in our political evolution, certainly adds a chapter to the romance of modern history."—*The Pall Mall Gazette.*

The London Correspondent of *The Bombay Gazette* writes to that journal :—

" I met a day or two ago the Secretary of the London Liberal Caucus, and I asked him what he thought of Mr. Dadabhai Naoroji's prospects. His reply was that the indefatigable Parsee candidate had an even chance of defeating Captain Penton, who though a large owner of property in the district, and an open-handed supporter of local charities, has given offence to the working classes by his uncompromising refusal to support the eight hours' movement. Mr. Dadabhai is, in regard to labour questions, very advanced ; in fact he is almost a socialist ; at any rate his sympathies are strongly with those gentlemen who, though they have not been able to secure much support for their own utopian schemes, may take credit for having largely contributed to bring about the new direction which politics are taking here and on the continent. Mr. Dadabhai's friends are working most energetically ; and as his friends include a goodly number of the fair sex, the ' sirens of the Primrose League ' have not it all their own way in Central Finsbury as they have in some other parts of the metropolis."

The London Correspondent of the *Morning Post* writes : —" If there is one elected representative of the people who is sorry that his share in the electoral battle was crowned with victory, that one must be the Parsee gentleman who was chosen by East Finsbury. The poor man is deluged with invitations to such an extent that the postman's knock must strike terror to his soul, and demon of dyspepsia must perpetually dog his footsteps. Even if his appetite for flattery was as insatiable as that of a professional beauty and his digestion outrivalled that of the ostrich in its strength, he would not be able to enjoy the floods of congratulation and of public and private hospitality that are being poured upon him, because he is not quite sure that he is entitled to them, or to speak more correctly whether his right to receive these honours will long remain undisputed. The thought of the narrow majority by which he lost East Finsbury oftimes makes Captain Penton inclined to reject the advice of his counsellors and petition for a scrutiny, and while this thought continues to haunt the brain of his defeated adversary, Mr. Naoroji can feel but little of that comfort which springs from a sense of safety. Nor are weariness of mind and distress of stomach and insecurity of position the only things that the elected of Finsbury has to suffer. The rumour that the native princes of India had forwarded him a cheque for £300,000 as a substantial token of their pleasure in his success has caused him more misery than all the rest put together. As soon as the report was set afloat, begging letters began to pour in upon him from all sorts of sources. It was impossible to reply to these epistles separately, for they were in number like unto the sands of the seashore, so Mr. Naoroji notified his correspondents, through the medium of the press, that both they and he had been the victims of a hoax. This statement, however, had no appreciable effect upon the people for whose information it was published. Letters asking for help, letters pointing out the duty of almsgiving, and letters naming institutions and charities upon which his supposititious cash ought, in the opinion of the writers, to be bestowed still continued to come in, and I hear that these are now being supplemented by letters of reproach and rebuke from disappointed applicants, who have either not seen his printed reply to their supplications, or else have chosen to disbelieve the denial that it contained. Truly, the first Indian Member of Parliament is being made to pay a heavy penalty for his popularity."

"That remarkably mixed party (the Gladstonians) has the privilege of adding to its assorted ranks a fervent socialist in Mr. John Burns and a Parsee gentleman in Mr. Dadabhai Naoroji."—*The Standard.*

"No fair-minded Conservative will complain that her Majesty's Indian subjects should have a representative at the Imperial Legislature of their own race ; the misfortune is that Mr. Naoroji should have obtained his seat at the expense of a Unionist."—*The Morning Advertiser.*

"A short, slight man of contemplative cast of countenance, the 'deep eyes of a Hindoo', and a smile that would charm a bee from a honey-pot."—*The Evening News.*

MR. DADABHAI PARADING HIS WEALTH.

An Illusion.

The following highly imaginative paragraph appeared in one of the newspapers :—

"Mr. Dadabhai Naoroji" receives Congratulatory Thanks from Indian Potentates.

A Library for Finsbury.

"Mr. Dadabhai Naoroji, the newly-elected Liberal M.P. for Finsbury, has, according to a Dalziel correspondent, received within the last three days thirteen telegrams from different Maharajahs of India transferring to him sums varying from £500 to £5,000, in all £28,000, as an acknowledgment and encouragement of his political services. The Maharajah of Hyderabad has placed at his disposal a sum of £10,000 in addition to the above for the purpose of enabling Mr. Naoroji to establish a memorial of some kind, a monument, a public library, or some philanthropic work in his constituency."

Other papers followed suit. For instance, we have the *Echo* as follows :—

"Mr. Naoroji is not showing remarkable wisdom in flashing the wealth of India before the eyes of the British electorate. Since his election for Central Finsbury, he has received thirteen telegrams from as many Maharajahs of India, transmitting sums varying from £500 to £5,000, making in all £28,000, to pay the expenses of his election, and an additional sum of £10,000 from the Maharajah of Hyderabad to enable Naoroji to establish a permanent memorial in the division of his victory. Here we have £38,000 to assist in the return, and to signallize an electoral success.

"There is more purse-pride than wisdom in this display of riches. Central Finsbury abounds in needy people. And when £38,000 are paraded so soon after the election, many persons will, naturally enough, ask how much of it was promised and expended before the election. Should Mr. Naoroji present himself for re-election, as probably he may soon have an opportunity to do, the electorate will, naturally enough, look out for windfalls, as the candidate and his cause will be obscured by the shower of Maharajahs' contributions varying from £500 to £5,000. The Member for Central Finsbury will, in the circumstances, carry with him less rather than more moral force on account of Indian money poured into his lap."

And the *Globe* followed in a similar strain :—

"On the other hand rich and rare are the gifts that his election has brought to Mr. Naoroji, and we are somewhat at a loss to know why these Eastern potentates show so much grateful enthusiasm at the entrance that has been effected into the British Parliament by a gentleman who is not of their blood, nor of their religion. It can hardly be that the Maharajah of Hyderabad is really honoured and flattered by the introduction of a Parsee into a distant body of Englishman. Mr. Naoroji is as much an alien to the Indian Prince who has sent him presents as an Englishman would be. What then is the meaning of this outburst of gratitude? Are these gifts the outcome of their affection, or are they sent as means of propitiation? And, if so, why do Maharajahs wish to propitiate Mr. Naoroji? No doubt their idea of a member of Parliament is derived from intercourse with Mr. Kipling's ' Pagett, M.P.,' and they look with justifiable dread towards a Parsee ' Pagett.' "

Mr. Naoroji contradicted these statements in a letter sent to all the London dailies in these terms :—

" With reference to the statement in your issue of yesterday, that I have received telegrams and £38,000 from India, will you kindly allow me to inform your readers that though it is true that I have received many telegrams since my election, I have not received any money from India."

But the *Echo* pursued its own strain with persistent ungenerousness :—

" A man must not always tell all, for that were folly ; but what a man says should be what he thinks ; otherwise 'tis knavery. No doubt Mr. Naoroji has been informed of the big mistake he made in parading the wealth that was poured into his lap by the Maharajahs of India. He writes to us to say that ' though it is true I have received many telegrams since my election, I have not received any money from India.' It should be remembered that the sums promised him were specified. He does not attempt to contradict or correct any statement made. He merely says he has not received any money from India. Of course not, and for the best of all reasons. There has been insufficient time since his election to receive anything from India but telegrams. But Mr. Naoroji in no way improves his position by his explanation, but rather makes it more dubious. There is an oriental obliquity in his statement which will not raise him in the esteem of the British public for courage and candour. Though he has not received the promised money, he will in due time. Dalziel's agency says that the report in reference to the money is perfectly true, and will be publicly verified before long. Mr. Naoroji cannot help having money poured upon him by Indian Princes, but he can help making a parade of it; and when finding he had made a mistake, there was no necessity that he should seek shelter behind equivocation."

COMMENTS ON MR. NAOROJI'S MAIDEN SPEECH IN PARLIAMENT.

The London correspondent of the *Bombay Gazette* writes :—

Mr. Naoroji made his maiden speech on Tuesday night, and though he spoke to a rather limited audience—it was not generally known that he intended to take part in the No Confidence debate—he was listened to with close attention, and when he resumed his seat members flocked round him to offer their congratulations. During the earlier part of the evening he had been modestly sitting on the back benches, but just before he spoke he moved down to the second row, immediately behind the front Opposition bench. Among the members present at the time was the principal Liberal whip and right-hand man of Mr. Gladstone. Judging from his appearance Mr. Arnold Morley seems satisfied with Mr. Naoroji's *début*. Mr. Labouchere was also in the House, and in order better to hear the new member crossed over to a seat on the Ministerial side. The common practice here is to put the emphasis on the second syllable of his name. The speaker, in calling upon Mr. Naoroji, pronounced his name correctly, exactly as it would be pronounced in Bombay. As this was the first time that the voice of an Asiatic had been heard within the walls of Parliament, it is natural that Mr. Naoroji's utterances, though comparatively brief, should have attracted considerable notice. The *Times* rather sarcastically observes that Mr. Naoroji dilated with radiant *naïvette* on the splendour of his victory in Central Finsbury, and owing doubtless to the reluctance of the speaker to pull up a new member whose inexperience called for special indulgence was allowed to conclude without saying one word on the vote of " want of confidence." The *Standard*, the *Morning Post*, and the *Morning Advertiser* make no special reference to the

speech. The Unionist *Daily Telegraph* remarks :—" An
eloquent and fervent recruit to the Opposition ranks arrived
in the person of Mr. Dadabhai Naoroji, whose somewhat
ambiguous references to the terms of Her Majesty's Speech
were atoned for by the enthusiasm and earnestness which
carried him along." The Tory *Globe* says :—" Mr. Naoroji
delivered a remarkable harangue about India, full of
Oriental expressions of gratitude to the English people for
giving him an opportunity of appearing at Westminster."
The *St. James's Gazette* observes :—" Mr. Dadabhai Naoroji
is a new member, and in a way a distinguished stranger,
and for such there is always indulgence. Consequently the
worthy member for Central Finsbury was permitted
without interruption from the chair or benches to deliver a
highly decorous and very nicely expressed little lecture on
England and her great dependency, which would have been
very much in place at a meeting of the Anglo-Indian Association"—whatever that may be—" or the Zenana Mission."
I suppose the writer means Zenana Missionary Society.
He adds :—" The sentiments were praiseworthy, and Mr.
Naoroji speaks pleasantly with an excellent choice of language. But what his speech had to do with the question before
the House, nobody in the least understood." The wonder-
fully facetious gentleman who writes Parliamentary gup
for the *Manchester Examiner* (Liberal Unionist) discourses
on the subject with admirable taste and felicity. Here is
what this humourist and stylist says :—" Mr. Dadabhai
Naoroji, whom the wits of the House have for convenience
of pronunciation already converted into Mr. Narrow Majority "—the wits of the House then are three weeks behind
the fair—" and Mr. Dab-in-the-Eye Yo No, made his maiden
speech in the delights of the sylvan dinner hour "—Why
sylvan ?—" and it proved to be a treat indeed. Mr. Naoroji
talked sententiously of our great and glorious empire and
reminding us that we had treated India badly a hundred
years ago, rather grimly or, perhaps, one ought to say dark-
ly hinted, that he himself was a result of that treatment.
What all this had to do with the No Confidence Trick, no
one seemed able to say, and the speaker mercifully did not
lift his slumbering head to inquire." I do not think that
Mr. Peel's head was slumbering ; but that of the *Manchester
Examiner's* correspondent evidently was, judging from the
foregoing quotation. So much for the Conservative Press ;
now for the Liberal papers. The *Daily News* in its leading

article describes the speech as "graceful and dignified," but in another column says it was delivered under depress- ing circumstances. The House of Commons' "dinner hour" is always depressing, but as I know from conversation with many members it would have been less depressing on this occasion if Mr. Naoroji with excessive modesty had not withheld from his friends his intention to speak. The gallery man of the *Daily Chronicle* alludes to Mr. Naoroji's plea for India as "gracefully irrelevant and quite touching." In the editorial column of the same paper the following appears:—"To Mr. Naoroji will belong the distinction of being the first of the newly-elected Liberal London members to address the new Parliament. The hon. member delivered his maiden speech last night, and a very effective little address it was; it had the merit of being not too long and was listened to with great attention by a House which, considering it was near the middle of the dinner hour, was fairly well attended." The writer adds that Mr. Naoroji spoke very carefully and deliberately and in a fine sonorous voice. The disappointment of the new House at Mr. Naoroji's lightness of complexion has been, the *Pall Mall* informs us, "absolutely profound. A witty Gladstonian summed it up by the remark 'Lord Salisbury has been at his old game—calling white black.' Mr. Naoroji himself was very favourably received last night, was so mildly moderate as to disappoint the House even more than his colour." The *Star* says that no one will grudge Mr. Naoroji his graceful speech, although it had no reference to the subject discussed. Mr. Naoroji will, for the first time, exemplify the close connection between this country and India by speaking on behalf of his fellow-countrymen in Parliament. We see that even the Tory journals are pleased that the scrutiny in Central Finsbury did not result in unseating him. He is a man whom all parties should wish to see in Parliament. The Parliamentary reporter of the *Manchester Guardian* points out that Mr. Naoroji's voice "is entirely free from foreign accent or phraseology" and says that he had "reason to be satisfied with the attitude of the House towards him." The representative of a Liverpool daily considers that the speech was very interesting to one "who knew its accent." He goes on to say :— "Mr. Naoroji has the fluency of his race. He has also in his nervousness an almost beseeching way, an apologetic tone, which he will probably lose in the strife of politics.

There were numbers who stayed to hear him and they were not disappointed." Finally the *Morning Leader*, one of the new half-penny papers, states that Mr. Naoroji created a very favourable impression. Now if the Parsee community are not after all this praise proud of their enterprising co-religionist, they must be hard to please. I have heard in the lobby a doubt expressed but by one gentleman only as to the wisdom of Mr. Naoroji intervening in a debate so soon after his election. In view of certain legal threats I suppose he thought that if he did not avail himself of this opportunity, he might possibly not have another. Should his Parliamentary career be cut short by what my friend, the London correspondent of the *Journal des Delats*, calls the "subtilites delaloi electorale anglaise" Mr. Naoroji will not have had a bad innings. He has assisted at the opening of a new Parliament by accompanying the speaker to the House of Lords when the Royal Message was read; taken part in an historical debate; voted in the largest division that has ever been recorded at Westminster; and if he lives until next Thursday will have the pleasure of sitting on the right of the chair as a supporter of Mr. Gladstone's Fourth Ministry. Both in the House and its precincts, Mr. Naoroji is the observed of all observers.

A PARSEE IN PARLIAMENT.

TO THE EDITOR OF THE *Morning Post*.

Sir,—The election of Mr. Naoroji for Finsbury has given rise to the idea in some places that he represents the people of India. Far from it. Mr. Naoroji is a Parsee, a race as alien to India as a Russian Jew in Whitechapel is to England—a race of mere traders, none of whom ever drew a sword or pulled a trigger, either for or against us, a people who, if we left India, would be massacred to a man by the fighting races.—Yours, &c., RICHARD L. DASHWOOD, *Major-General*.

A Correspondent to *The National Observer*, writing on July 6, signing himself "P.," says:—"I was standing outside *The Daily News* Office to-night when Mr. Naoroji's election was announced. The general opinion seemed to be that it was a credit;—that the Liberals had been pulling up their socks and showing their policies;— that the new member was no blacker than yourself, but (if the truth were known, as genuine an Englishman as the rest of us; that he had been a Prime Minister somewhere abroad; and finally, that (as he was as good as Salisbury himself, and could consequently look him in the face on the floor of the House) he was just the man we wanted to represent the poor slaves who run about in India pursued by certain blokes with whips and bludgeons. It was felt to be inherently improbable that there were any such folk as Parsees. But, of course, if Mr. Naoroji insisted, he could always worship a box of matches or the clock tower. We were all for religious toleration. As for national prejudices or racial pride—such feelings were out of date."

From the London Letter to *The Hindu*, Madras.

A Conservative evening paper, published in London, tells Indians that if they desire anything in the shape of " a greater share in the administration of their country," they should remember what the Roman Emperor Nero would have done had he been asked for constitutional privileges by the Feudatories of the Roman Empire. " Nero would probably have made torches of them." The " them " referred to are the " tributaries " of Rome. Probably, the Conservative paper referred to individuals and not to countries. Indeed, he must have done so: it is not easy to understand how a country could have been made into a torch, but it is easy to understand how dark North Africans or fair Angles might have been dipped into oil, well covered with thoroughly naphtha-soaked garments, and then lighted " to make a Roman holiday." This then is the way in which a leading Conservative Journal alludes to the constitutional and reasonable demands of fellow subjects of the British people. Where Lord Salisbury calls Irishmen " Hottentots " and Mr. Naoroji, M.P., a " black man," the *Evening News and Post* talks of Nero's probable making torches of men, and ironically congratulates the Indian people " that they do not need

SUCH A GHASTLY BEACON FIRE

to indicate the safe course." The " safe course " for the Indians is not to ask for " a greater share in the administration of their country." If some orator at the Allahabad Congress should make this brutal observation the text for some very forcible remarks in December next, nobody need be surprised.

APPENDIX.

The Results of the Scrutiny.

(*From Reuter's Telegrams.*)

THE CENTRAL FINSBURY ELECTION.

LONDON, *November* 26.

Capt. Penton has withdrawn the charges against Mr. Dadabhai Naoroji and agreed to a scrutiny, which has been fixed to take place on 5th December, to decide the election.

THE CENTRAL FINSBURY ELECTION.

LONDON, *December* 13.

The scrutiny of voting papers in Central Finsbury is proceeding, and a number of alien votes have been disallowed on both sides. Mr. Dadabhai Naoroji at present has a majority of two. The scrutiny has been adjourned until Thursday.

THE CENTRAL FINSBURY SCRUTINY.

LONDON, *December* 14.

The scrutiny of voting papers at Central Finsbury was yesterday resumed. Mr. Dadabhai Naoroji last night was two votes ahead of Captain Penton.

LONDON, *December* 14.

After numerous votes had been disallowed on both sides, Captain Penton and Mr. Dadabhai Naoroji were level this morning; and after luncheon Captain Penton withdrew his petition, each side arranging to pay their own costs.

MR. DADABHAI NAOROJI'S ELECTION.

The *Bombay Gazette* writes:—The result of the scrutiny in Central Finsbury is a tie—a disappointment alike to Mr. Dadabhai Naoroji and Captain Penton. The latter (*sic*) retains the seat, but he has been condemned to see his majority of three first raised to five and then disappear altogether, leaving him on a level with his pertinacious rival. The costs of such prolonged proceedings are of course heavy, and no doubt both parties were glad to escape the risk of having to pay his opponent's costs in addition to his own. This risk was perilously near, for the rejection of another solitary vote on their side would have sufficed to double the sum which the loser would have to pay. They were well advised to say quits and close the scrutiny. It is to be regretted for his own sake that Captain Penton did not elect to withdraw the petition a little sooner, and thus earn a useful reputation for magnanimity to an opponent. Secure in his local influence as a proprietor of extensive house property in the borough, he might have consoled himself with the hope and even with the assurance that on a future occasion his supporters would take care that he was not left in a minority of three. The outward result of the recent polling, and so far as he was concerned it was an untoward result—it was attributed by his friends to surprise. Up to almost the last moment, two Liberals were in the field and the Conservatives deemed the issue of the election a foregone conclusion. They did not exert themselves to perfect their organisation, and when the second Liberal candidate withdrew in favour of Mr. Dadabhai, Captain Penton's friends found to their dismay that they had to fight not a disunited but a united party. Even under those discouraging circumstances, the Conservatives came within one vote of success. Mr. Schnadhorst will doubtless see in the closeness of the contest the justification for his foreboding that the perseverance of Mr. Dadabhai would cast the Liberals the seat. It has not done so, but Mr. Schandhorst's prediction came within an ace of unwelcome fulfilment. For this Parliament Mr. Dadabhai is not only member for India, but what is perhaps of some practical import, member for Central Finsbury. His vote will be on the side of the Government, whose majority, which had fallen to 38 under the influence of the earlier, has been raised by the result of the more recent election petitions to 44. Mr. Dadabhai is to be congratulated on retaining his seat even after he has lost his majority, the only member of this or we believe any other Parliament who has accomplished so remarkable a feat. The only analogue to it is that of the hero of the weird German tale who lost his shadow, but retained his substance. It is to be hoped that the tenacity which has proved too strong for Mr. Schnadhorst and Captain Penton alike, will enable Mr. Dadabhai, now that he has made good his footing in the House of Commons, to put to shame those who say, like Mr. Dicey, that no one can show a single instance in which Parliamentary interference in Indian matters ever did a halfpenny worth of good.

www.ingramcontent.com/pod-product-compliance
Lightning Source LLC
Chambersburg PA
CBHW030611270326
41927CB00007B/1121